The Pocket Book of
PROPAGATION

The Pocket Book of
PROPAGATION

Anita Guyton

Evans Brothers Limited London

Published by
Evans Brothers Limited
Montague House
Russell Square, London WC1B 5BX

Drawings by Bucken

First published 1981

British Library Cataloguing in Publication Data

Guyton, Anita
The pocket book of propagation.
1. Plant propagation
I. Title
631.5'3 SB119

ISBN 0-237-45556-0 PRA 7292

Composition by Filmtype Services Limited,
Scarborough, England.

Printed in Great Britain by
Richard Clay (The Chaucer Press) Ltd,
Bungay, Suffolk

Dedicated to dearest Ninian, who throughout the writing of this and other books has given me constant encouragement, and has supported me with great kindness, patience and understanding.

CONTENTS

1. FOREWORD

All gardeners adore talking about gardening in general, and their successes in particular, but few ever wish to discuss propagation. I believe it's the word 'propagation', which has an awful scientific ring to it, which deters many enthusiasts from experimenting more than they do. Yet, one doesn't need to be a botanist to understand how to grow things, and once you read these pages, you will quickly discover that the seemingly complicated growing techniques are really nothing like as difficult as you may think.

Knowing how to rear anything which grows will save you money, but what is even more important is that it will increase and intensify your enjoyment in gardening. It is possible that for the first time you will appreciate all the exciting and varying stages of growth, and all the pleasure in the multiplied beauty and splendour thereof will be entirely due to your own efforts. Just remember – 'Life itself is exciting, and exciting gardening is life itself!'

2. THE PSYCHOLOGY AND CARE OF PLANTS

I am an ardent gardener – indeed some would go further and say that my passion borders on the fanatical, which may well be true! Yet, of one thing I am quite certain. To have any degree of success with the rearing of any sort of living, breathing, and growing thing, whether it be a child, a pet, a favourite houseplant, or some special garden plant or shrub, one thing is essential. Apart from knowing the ordinary do's and don'ts involved, you must have a deep and basic understanding of the subject concerned.

When it comes to plants, I certainly don't mean you need the sort of mind which can memorise the needs of each individual, in much the same way as one would learn a poem by heart. No, I'm talking about something which I believe to be even more important than that, what I can only describe to you as plant psychology! Now, this may at first sound weird and way-out, but let me explain further: in order to succeed in propagating, perhaps by a stem cutting, or rearing a fine specimen from seed, you have first to overcome or avoid the problems which may beset them. Of course, being told how moist the compost should be, and all the 'musts' concerning light and warmth, etc., is essential if the operation is to be a success, but in many ways it's like having a cooking recipe which gives the necessary ingredients, without giving the quantities. Unfortunately, there is no sure way of measuring these 'contents' accurately, so, consequently, this is where your psychology comes into play.

Just for a moment, imagine yourself to be that tiny cutting or seed, and then you will have a far better and more accurate idea of how it will be faring. Once you are that much more conscious, and can sense that they have no roots through which to absorb moisture, then automatically you will be more wary about over-watering them. A certain amount of warmth is necessary, not only for the plant's top growth, but for its submerged and rooting cut end as well. However, artificial heating is not always necessary if the stems are snugly encased in a reasonably sized pot. Once you give it some thought, it won't be difficult to understand that an over-large pot, which has more than enough compost space for the rooting needs of the cutting, chills far more quickly than a pot with only a small compost area. So, even if your cutting is taken from a fairly rapid grower, always root it first in a pot which provides just sufficient space, no more, and then, later on, when it has rooted and is growing, it can be transferred to a one-size larger container. Remember, too, that plastic pots remain relatively warmer than the traditional clay pots, because the walls are not porous and cannot breathe. However, although this property of plastic pots is an advantage at times, it may prove the opposite if your previous failures were caused by a constantly over-wet compost. In that case, you should most certainly think twice about using them, because the compost contained within this non-porous wall does not dry out as quickly as clay, and unless you are especially careful, that old rotting problem could soon be back again.

Another important factor which should be considered when propagating any type of cutting is that plants not only feed via their roots but also breathe through their foliage. Once a section of stem or leaf has been severed from its rooted base, it cannot continue the process of drawing-up and absorbing moisture through the root channels. Yet the water already in the dismembered top section will continue to be expended, a process which must be prevented if the cutting is not to wilt. Fast-flagging and floppy cuttings rarely muster sufficient energy to put down new roots.

Now plants, especially those which originate from the tropical rain forests of the world, thrive in a humid atmosphere. Such close, moist conditions, however, must not be provided by a constantly wet and soggy compost for the reasons I have already mentioned, but the air surrounding the cutting must be contained in such a way that when the slight dampness from the rooting mixture rises, it envelopes the growing part and, equally importantly, any 'dewiness' which is exhaled by the cutting is retained and recycled back through the pores, thus keeping the limb vigorous.

Mini Greenhouses

There are many seeds and cuttings which will take quite easily, without any form of artificial bottom heating, but one very important point to remember is that they must always be provided with a moist and enclosed atmosphere if they are to survive. Quite often, many methods of propagating fail only because the surrounding air, though warm, is far too dry, which quickly causes the cuttings to dry out long before they have the opportunity to root.

However, don't believe that the problem will be cured by making the soil more wet. All this will do is add to the original difficulty, by causing ideal conditions for fungal diseases. A balance between an evenly damp compost, and a moist atmosphere, may be achieved in several simple and basically similar ways. A deepish fruit bowl, meat tray, or paté dish for example, can soon become the foundation of a mini greenhouse. First cover the bottom with approximately 5cm-7.5cms (2-3ins) of freshly washed coarse gravel, and then pour in a little water, so that it barely covers the floor and doesn't reach the top of the gravel. A few small pots of cuttings can then be placed on this base, and the whole covered with a sheet of transparent polythene. Because the water level is far below the base of the pots, the compost will not become any more damp than it was when you put them in. What the water will provide is a constantly humid environment which, being contained, cannot dry out. Some beads of moisture will collect under the covering, and these must never be allowed to remain – just sponge them away quickly.

The most frequently used method of all is simply to enclose any newly potted cuttings under a clean see-through polythene bag. Secure the open end tightly

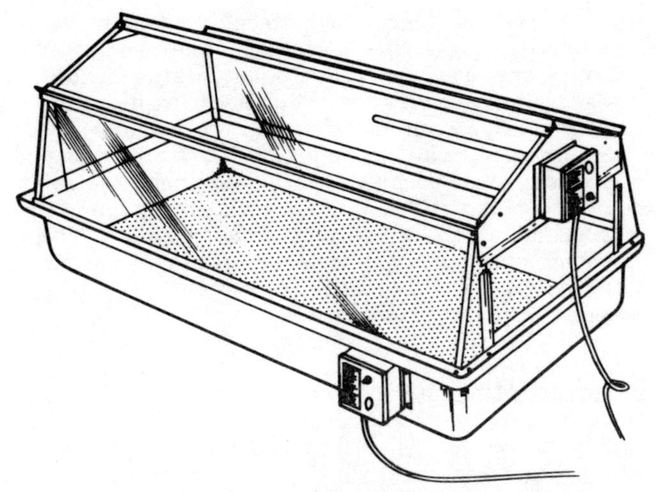

A propagating box.

around the pot, so that there is no flow of air, and you will have as near as you will get to a mini greenhouse. I often use this technique which is extremely effective, and if you stand the pots on a warm shelf, the seeds and cuttings will germinate and root readily, though not as quickly as when reared in a thermostatically controlled propagator.

The simplest propagators have no artificial means of heating, and are composed of two plastic sections which fit snugly together. They work on the same principle as the polythene cover treatment which I mentioned earlier. An electrically heated model, with a soil warming cable, will provide cuttings with the desired bottom heat. If you have a little knowledge and a carpenter's know-how, you can make a fairly elaborate or just a simple propagating box at only a fraction of the shop price. The necessary electric cables may be purchased from the makers or sellers of greenhouses, and because the soil temperature in a propagator takes a while to drop, a thermostat isn't vital.

If, however, you intend to buy a ready-made propagator, I always believe it pays dividends to wait until you can afford a good one which has both soil- and air-warming cables and is not only thermostatically controlled, but has a misting device as well. A misting apparatus produces a fine spray, particularly beneficial if you wish to raise a number of slow-rooting, and hardwood cuttings which under ordinary conditions might quickly flag and fail, and it is a must when it comes to raising very delicate strains. Many tender varieties need to be over-wintered, and this is when the air-warming cable comes in handy. With a propagator which will provide a controlled temperature of 13°–27°C (55°–81°F), there is no field of propagation in which you cannot indulge.

Rooting Mixture

Any gardener knows that a good, open, loamy soil is the best growing medium of all. Yet, when it comes to propagating seeds, and raising young seedlings or unrooted cuttings, it's always best to play safe and leave the garden soil exactly where it is! However rich and crumbly a soil may be, it's no use even attempting to rear any vulnerable young plants unless the mixture is absolutely disease and pest free, and the only way to ensure this is to use a sterilised and pre-packed potting compost, which also contains all the necessary plant nutrients,

A seed compost, such as Levington's or John Innes is perfectly formulated for growing seeds, and may be used straight from the polythene packing. It is also suitable for rooting cuttings, but you will find that it is much more effective and economical if you add one part of clean sand to every three parts of seed compost. Sand and/or peat is a good rooting medium but it contains no nutrients on which young plants can feed. Therefore, as soon as it has served its purpose, and the cuttings and seeds have rooted and germinated, they must be repotted into a more suitable compost such as Levington's or John Innes No. 1.

Then later, when they are larger and more hardy, they can either be repotted in the No. 2 mixture, or bedded out into a fertile and porous soil.

3. SEEDS

The old saying that there's many a slip 'twixt the cup and the lip has no more apt application than to the germination of seeds. From the first sowing, through all the varying stages to the final planting out, the road to success is littered with pitfalls, largely due to the fact that we are inclined to forget that each seed contains a life, which needs to be cared for if it is eventually to develop into a strong and independent young plant. We can all understand what seeds are, but it is very easy to lose sight of their ability to reproduce visible life.

When plants grow naturally, the fertilisation of a flower is frequently performed by birds, butterflies, bees, and other insects. In their search for nectar, they inadvertently become dusted with pollen from the part of the flower which contains the male anther, and this pollen becomes transferred to the ovary which is contained in the female section of the flower. The same principle applies also to cultivated varieties, except that cross-pollination is not left entirely to nature but is frequently carried out by human hands; the resultant seeds often combine the characteristics of both parents. Although seeds can vary slightly, especially when the parents have a mixed ancestry (hence the beginnings of a new strain) they usually run fairly true to type.

Seeds vary enormously in shape and size, from tiny, almost dust-like seeds, to large, hard-coated, stones like the avocado. When dormant, some seeds such as the calceolarias only survive a short while before they lose their strength, whilst others can last for months or even years.

Whatever the differences between certain seeds, they have some things in common. Each one contains a vital food store, much of which is used up whilst they are germinating, and before they make any sizeable roots at all. None will start to sprout until they are provided with the external conditions which are conducive to growth. Some of the slow-germinating and hard-shelled seeds may require a little additional encouragement to germinate, and there are several simple means of speeding up what would otherwise be a slow process.

Varieties like sweet-pea seeds are best chipped with a small, sharp knife, so that only the outer casing is scarred. Peach, plum, and almond stones, with their almost impenetrable casings, and slow-sprouting types such as roses, alpines, and hollies, should be given the cold treatment, which is generally known as stratification. This entails subjecting them to extremely frosty conditions, when the low temperatures encourage the hard external shells to soften, and the seeds within become more likely to react to any subsequent and noticeable warmth – hence germination is more readily achieved. The seed pods and stones, which must be gathered only when they are completely ripe, should be buried in a box of dry sand. After covering them, place thin chicken wire or fine netting on top to protect them from birds, squirrels and mice, and put the box out-of-doors on a bed of loose bricks or rubble in an open position throughout the coldest months. After about twelve months, sieve the sand, and remove the mixed seeds. The fruit stones may be planted immediately, but the seeds of such as roses, hollies, and yews must be removed from their soft pulpy skins by hand, before sowing them in the usual way.

Of course, gardeners have been known to improvise necessary conditions when they are not available naturally, and in this case you should first soak the seeds for several hours in tepid water, and then put them in the refrigerator.

Very tiny types of seed, and the larger ones of camellias and magnolias do not keep well (magnolia seeds have a somewhat oily texture), and so should be sown as soon as possible. The skins of stored peas and runner beans can become very dry, and those of you who as children were the targets or the owners of pea shooters, will know exactly how bullet-like they can feel. These will always benefit from a two-day soaking in water, which will not only soften and cause them to swell, but also urge them to sprout more quickly than if left to their own devices.

Sowing Seeds

Seeds may be sown in all types of containers – clay or plastic flower pots, boxes or even ice-cream cartons with a few holes in the base, but if you wish to germinate more than just a handful then a seed tray of either wood or plastic becomes necessary. If the container has no drainage holes, or is somewhat deep, then a layer of newly washed crocks such as stones, broken bricks, or pieces of clay pot, should cover the floor to a depth of at least 2.5cm (1in).

If you use a seed tray, fill it to within 1.25cm (½in) of the top with either pure seed compost, or a mixture of 2 parts of J.I.P. No. 1 to 1 part of gritty sand and 1 part of peat and firm it down lightly. Spray the mixture so that it is moist, but not soggy, and allow it to drain thoroughly. Very tiny seeds need only to be scattered finely over the compost and left uncovered, but if they are one of the slow-germinating varieties, then play safe by treating them to a fungicidal seed dressing. Unlike the really fine seeds, the larger varieties need a top-covering of compost equal to the size of the seeds. If a seed or stone is approximately 1.25cm (½in) thick, then the top covering should not exceed 1.25cm (½in) above the seed. The same rule also applies to the pelleted kinds, which are ordinary seeds, coated to make handling and planting easier. The coating frequently contains a fungicide, which gives them a double protection from any early bothers. Of course, there are exceptions to every general rule, and broad beans, garden peas, and runner beans are three of them. They are inclined to move towards the surface as they germinate, and so need to be set somewhat deeper at nearer 6.25cm (2½in).

The tray should then be covered with a sheet of glass, but I have found that transparent, self-adhesive

Pricking out a seedling.

polythene, which one normally uses in the kitchen, is just as effective and often more practical. Condensation will collect on the underside of this lid, and it must be wiped away without too much delay, for if it is left to fall on the seeds, they will be harmed by damping-off disease. (This is a fungus which is inclined to attack seedlings growing in over-wet, over-hot, and over-crowded conditions, and infected plants should be treated with a Cheshunt compound, captan, or a thiram seed dressing.)

Seeds need little light, and so the glass or polythene should be covered with brown paper or newspaper, but only until the seedlings have appeared above the soil. They do need warmth, but should never be exposed to direct sunshine. A few days after the minute seedlings are visible, the glass can also be removed, and when they have grown several leaves apiece, and are large enough to handle safely, they can be carefully pricked out with a flat V-shaped stick. Either pot them individually into small pots, or transfer several at a time into one large container, and set them at a distance of 6.25cm (2½in) from each other. In each case the pots must contain a bottom covering of crocks to ensure good drainage, before being topped up to just below the rim, with either John Innes or Levingtons No. 1 compost. From this point on, the soil must never be allowed to dry out completely, and the growing plants will need plenty of good light, and a certain amount of both warmth and fresh air.

Those plants which are intended eventually for an outdoor display, will need first to be hardened off. This involves exposing them, in short doses at a time, to slightly cooler conditions, more air and more light, until they are sufficiently strong and hardy to be transplanted outside safely. Perennials and biennials will need to be transferred to progressively larger pots as they grow. Before planting them out, move them to a cold frame or unheated greenhouse, and after a few weeks, when they have become acclimatised, they can be placed outside with only a cloche for protection. Eventually, when all likelihood of a severe frost has passed, the cloches can be removed, and the plants safely bedded-out.

Outdoor sowing

The successful sowing of seeds directly out-of-doors is only possible after the soil has been well prepared, and the preparation will obviously vary according to the types of plants and vegetables you wish to grow. However, certain basic essential work must start in the autumn, when the texture of heavy soils can be lightened by adding a quantity of peat, sand and weathered ashes, whilst sandy or infertile areas can be enriched with well-decayed compost. Dig the latter in well, turn it, and leave it for a frost to do the work.

In the spring it will need to be firmed and raked several times, until the tilth is fine and stone-free, and only then can sowing begin. Seeds can be sown either in drills, or broadcast (which means sowing them, not in lines, but at even intervals over a given area) and the choice very much depends on your preference. Never set the seeds too closely together, because this will only result in weak and lanky seedlings, all fighting for some space, and necessitate drastic thinning-out. Always try to follow the planting instructions on the packet carefully, and, after lightly raking over the soil, immediately label each drill and newly planted plot clearly, otherwise you may well forget what is where. Unless the soil and atmosphere is very dry, it is unnecessary to water a new seed bed, but if you do, use warm to hot water, and not cold. The heat and damp will encourage the seeds to germinate more quickly.

Seeds of Shrubs and Trees

One day, when you are just pottering in the garden and enjoying all the beautiful things around you, perhaps you will fancy trying your hand at rearing a favourite shrub or tree from seed. Nowadays, when someone wants a particular variety, they jump into the car and drive to the nearest gardening centre, and although it is wonderful to know that such expertise in producing fine shrubs is so close at hand, it is certainly nothing like as rewarding as growing your own.

I know, all too well, that the method I suggest is one of the slowest ways of rearing any tree or shrub to adulthood, but you will discover that it is much more satisfying than buying one ready to plant. When you have such a challenge – and after all this is to a large degree what gardening is all about, Nature versus Man, – which could take many months of your life before you see the end result, don't you think that such excitement is thoroughly invigorating? I know I do!

The seeds of certain trees and shrubs can take anything up to two years to germinate, whilst the berried varieties, such as the holly (*Ilex*), normally need between six and twelve months to dry before they are ready to be sown. Roses can be propagated from seed, but, depending on the variety, it may be perhaps two, sometimes even three years before they produce mature, flowering bushes, and the resulting offspring can be guaranteed to grow true only if you pollinate them yourself, by hand. The seeds or hips should be subjected to the cold treatment described on p. 16 for at least twelve months. When this long waiting time has elapsed, you can of course try to separate the seeds from the sand by passing them through a fine sieve, but I much prefer to scatter both the seeds and sand together, except when it contains hips. These must be first collected and opened and the seeds must be extracted. The time for action will depend on the types of seed, but generally this is around early spring, when they should be sown in pans of seed compost and placed in a cold or garden frame.

Once the small seedlings have several leaves and are large enough to be handled safely, they can be set into a protected part of the garden in the spring of the following year. However, I usually play safe and cover mine with cloches until all signs of frost have passed.

Propagating Bulbous Plants from Seed

When we want to grow indoor or outdoor flowering bulbs we usually pop round to our nearest gardening shop or centre and obtain all we need in a few moments. Once planted, these bulbs provide us with a delightful and often fairly long flowering display within a year, depending, of course, on where and when we set them. But what about those already well-established annually blooming crocuses, hippeastrums, hyacinths, lilies, and tulips, some of which produce their own seeds quite naturally?

If you are adventurous it is a pity to waste these seeds. Of course, it is far quicker and probably much easier simply to detach the offsets and grow them on to full maturity, as I explain on page 88. This means of rearing new bulbs by offsets is very reliable because the new plants always have the characteristics of the parent. But you cannot expect the same from seed which has been naturally pollinated from perhaps one of many hybrid varieties, and this makes the whole venture exciting, because the resulting plants may embody a number of surprises. For instance, a resultant freak, which in no way resembles its parents, may perhaps bear one or a number of strong characteristics from one or two of its four grandparents.

You can see that the progeny possibilities are endless, and that the whole project could prove fascinating, especially if you start hand-pollinating varieties of your own choice. However, that is another matter. Here, I hope to deal with the rearing of some bulbous plants from seed.

Crocuses

The seedlings of crocuses normally take from two to four

years to reach flowering maturity, and there's no way of knowing whether the eventual blooms will prove interestingly different or not. There is only the one long way to find out, and that is to collect the seed capsules which appear on short stems during June and July. Ideally, they should be gathered just when the capsules start to split open preparatory to revealing and scattering the ripe seeds within. Then they should be sown 1.25cm (½in) deep in pots of seed compost, and placed in a cold yet protected spot, either in an unheated greenhouse or a cold frame.

Keep the compost comfortably moist, but otherwise leave the seeds exactly where they are for about two years. When the spring of the third year comes, they can be planted into a prepared bed in the garden, and then you can wait, watch, and wonder!

Hippeastrums

If pollination has occurred quite naturally between two hippeastrums, one or both being a hybrid, then there's no knowing what changes in colour or other characteristics may occur in the resulting offspring. But if hand-pollination has been performed, involving two hippeastrums of the same strain, and they themselves are not the result of any inter-breeding, then the resulting seeds should produce blooms with the same colour charateristics as the parents. Remember, it takes at least three years for any young seedlings to bear flowers, so you will need plenty of patience.

The seeds must be gathered and potted-up when ripe, and as near to the beginning of spring as possible. Sow them 2.5cm (1in) apart, and sprinkle on enough compost just to cover them. Place them in a light but shaded position away from the sun, and keep the compost moist. Given an even temperature of 64°F (18°C), they should germinate quite readily, and as soon as the seedlings have several leaves apiece and can be easily pricked out, they should be transplanted singly into 6.25cm (2½in) pots containing J.I.P. No. 1 compost.

Subsequently, they will become root-bound and outgrow their pots, and each time this happens they must be repotted into a one-size larger pot. When they have finally reached a 5-inch pot, they will need to be repotted into J.I.P. No. 2 compost. Throughout this entire growing period, the compost must be kept evenly moist, and only when the bulb has flowered for the first time, and the foliage started to shrivel and die, can the adult hippeastrums be treated in the usual way and the compost allowed to dry out.

Hyacinths

Most of the flowering varieties of hyacinth which we buy for indoor or outdoor planting are propagated from offsets (see p. 89). However, they can be grown from seed but if you want to have a go, it must be emphasised that the resulting blooms are rarely, if ever, superior to the large-headed and deliciously fragrant heads produced by the shop bulbs.

If you find the prospect attractive, scatter the ripe seeds finely in boxes containing moistened seed compost, or J.I.P. No. 1. Cover with a sheet of clear glass, and keep them in an unheated greenhouse where they can be left undisturbed for twelve months. Then they can be transplanted individually into pots of J.I.P. No. 1, and grown on in the normal way. Don't expect a glorious show of colour too quickly – they take anything up to six years to reach flowering maturity!

Liliums

Lilium seeds, like those of certain other plants we've already mentioned, do not automatically run true to type, and this especially applies to the hybrid strains. In addition to that, some seeds are also inclined to take their time, and it might be as long as a year and a half before a seedling finally rears its little head. So don't let them fool you, as they have me on more than one occasion, into believing that they are never going to germinate. Obviously some won't – after all, every gardener has his failures – but do give them plenty of time.

On the other hand, there are some, like the lime-hating *L. formosanum* with its white flowering blooms, the outsides of which are sometimes tinged with brown or mauve, which are very accommodating indeed. When reared under glass, they produce the first of their 16.5cm (6½in) long trumpet-shaped flowers within a matter of only six months. The very lovely orange-flowering *L. davidii*, from China, is another strain which, though short-lived, can easily be reared from seed each year. And there are still more, such as the Korean *L. leichtlinii*, the hardy *L. mackliniae* with whitish-purple bell-shaped heads, and yet again, the *L. martagon* with curved reddish-purple blooms, which is probably better known by its more common name of Turk's-cap Lily.

The seeds of liliums which are to be both propagated and then cultivated under glass, should be sown about 2.5cm (1in) apart and 1cm (½in) deep, in boxes of seed compost. Provided with a steady warmth, they frequently germinate within three months, and then they can be removed to a cold frame for a further six to eight weeks, to be hardened off before being returned to the greenhouse.

Seeds which are ultimately destined to adorn your garden borders should be sown as soon as the seeds are ripe, as near to early autumn as possible, in boxes of seed compost. Put them 23cm (9in) down but still 2.5cm (1in) apart, and then place them outside in the cold frame. When the seedlings appear (they look like little green loops) they should be pricked out and repotted into boxes of J.I.P. No. 1 compost, at a depth and distance of 5cm (2in).

When all chances of frost have passed, and the weather is suitably mild, they can be transplanted out of doors into a specially prepared bed. There, they must be allowed to mature for three years, after which they can at last be moved to a permanent position, where the soil is both quick-draining and rich in leaf-mould and peat.

Tulips

During the summer, a couple of years back, I had a great deal of fun preparing and planting seed from some of my tulips. The seed pods started to yellow in the summer, and this is the perfect time to harvest them. They were duly picked, stored in a paper-lined box and placed in a warm cupboard to dry. When the pods were ready, they split and scattered many ripe seeds. I sowed them thinly in boxes of seed compost, and placed them in the greenhouse, although a conservatory will do equally well so long as it is cool and unheated.

Whilst the seedlings are germinating, and right up to the time their foliage dies, the compost must be kept moist. Then all watering must cease until late the following winter, when the leaves will start to sprout. Then watering can be resumed safely. The process should be repeated during the second year, and when the foliage dies off in the autumn, and watering is withheld, the plantlets can be replanted outside into drills. Pick a warm sunny position where the soil is quick-draining, and subsequently treat them exactly like mature bulbs, by lifting and storing them each year. They can flower any time from the third to the seventh year onwards.

Sowing a Lawn

When I came to write this section on the sowing of grass seed, I realised that such very important preparatory steps as ensuring ample and adequate drainage, and levelling the ground were too far removed from the subject of propagation to be given much space. However, I must remind you that these preparations are essential.

When it comes to dealing with any kind of grass seed, the treatment of the soil before sowing plays an integral part in determining whether your finished effort will afford you a lush carpet of rich and healthy greenery, or a threadbare and patchy plot. The soil should always be prepared some months before sowing, and any which is inclined to be somewhat tacky and difficult to work, can be greatly improved with ash from your indoor grate or garden bonfire. Mix a good quantity thoroughly with some sharp sand, and then spread evenly over the surface area before digging the top-soil. Now that central heating seems to be taking over from the more sociable open coal fires in most homes, soot is becoming a scarce commodity, but when it is available, this too should be worked in with the ash and sand. Together, they will go a long way toward making the soil more pliable and easier to work.

Ordinary light soils can of course be enriched with well-rotted stable manure, but if there are no riding schools nearby, you can use one of the many artificial lawn fertilisers now available, or alternatively work in plenty of well-rotted garden manure from the compost heap. Finally, treat the plot to a sprinkling of lime at approximately 100g (4oz) to the square yard. This will prove extremely beneficial in the long run. Once the entire surface has been dug, you should alternately rake and roll it, removing any large stones and pebbles as you go, until you produce the ideal surface with a fine, loose, and crumbly tilth.

For quick results, seed may be sown in early spring, but many gardeners including myself prefer to wait until late summer, having left the soil to lie fallow during the spring and summer months. There are several good and practical reasons for this preference, one being that due to the somewhat unpredictable climate in many countries there just might be a heatwave and a drought. A scorching sun, coupled with a lack of moisture, is not the ideal beginning for any lawn! Whereas during the autumn the rainfall is more likely to be reliable and regular. Another good reason is that I prefer to lay the bare earth open so that any weeds which germinate once the warmer weather arrives can be removed easily; this is not so simple when they are hidden and partially protected by new grass.

When you come to buy your seed, it will be as well to let the seedsman have a small sample of soil before you decide on the blend. This will give him a good idea of the most suitable mixture to offer you. Frequently, the fine and more expensive blends are reserved for light to medium grades of soil, whilst the coarser mixtures, which often contain rye grass, are far better suited to heavier soils and lawns which are specifically intended for regular ball games. They need to be far more durable and hard-wearing.

Always tread the ground down thoroughly before sowing the seed by hand, and choose a windless day. To help ensure a fairly regular distribution of seed, it is a great help to use string to divide the area into strips, and then treat each piece individually, with the required amount of seed. To achieve the perfect closely knit lawn, you must allow approximately 60g of seed to every square metre (2oz to every square yard). I realise that many owners of large town gardens are inclined to skimp, using only about half this amount, but the resulting lawn is certainly never as thick and springy. The noticeable difference really does not justify the meagre saving. When you have finished sowing, rake over the area lightly so that the seed is barely covered, and finish off by firming the ground with a medium-weight roller.

Birds can be a real nuisance while you're waiting for the first signs of green, but they can be deterred if you insert canes or stakes at regular intervals, each side of the seeded patch. From these canes, attach lengths of black cotton in a criss-cross fashion, and pull it taut. It is an effective dissuasion in which birds don't feel inclined to get entwined!

Never be tempted to cut the young grass until it is at least two inches high, and then I would only feel inclined just to top it with a sickle or shears. If you give the grass this gentle treatment during the first four or five cuttings, you will give it a much better chance to become well established.

4. PROPAGATING FROM SPORES

Anyone who has ever delighted in the numerous varieties of outdoor fern such as the Hard Shield Fern (*Polystichum aculeatum*) which has deep green and glossy pinnate fronds, the Buckler Ferns, like the pale yellowish-green Crested Buckler Fern (*Dryopteris cristata*) and the Rigid Buckler Fern (*Dryopteris villarsi*) with its olive-green fronds, will surely be eager to try their skills at propagating these and many other gorgeous strains from spores. You and your gardening companions will almost certainly have lots growing outside, but the comparatively simple yet ingenious method of plant procreation is by no means limited to outdoor horticulture.

On the contrary, those who grow ferns in the greenhouse or conservatory, and perhaps keep the odd few as houseplants, can also try their hand. Varieties like the Birds Nest Fern (*Asplenium nidus*), with bright shuttlecock-like undivided fronds, the Stag Horn Fern which has deep green antler-shaped 'leaves', and the more typical-looking ferns like the Japanese Holly Fern (*Polystichum falcatum*) and the Sword Fern (*Nephrolepis*), all lend themselves to this most thrilling of all forms of propagation.

Ferns are termed neuter plants, for they haven't the same means of reproducing as flowering and seeding varieties. Because of this, nature has endowed them with the ability to reproduce hundreds of spores on the undersides of their fronds. This is why, in the wild, adult ferns can frequently be seen surrounded by numerous smaller second and third generation plants. For, once the spores turn brown and fall (if they are not transported by the wind, as frequently happens) they quickly make their roots near at home. Each of these spores contains fine, dust-like micro-seeds, which, when set in favourable con-

The spores of a fern.

ditions, produce tiny flat green scales known as *prothalli*, and these contain both male and female genes. The active male organisms contain cells which float across to pollinate the eggs of the female cells, and this union of the two cells activates fertilisation which results in the birth of a minute baby fern. Although the understanding of these minuscule workings is not essential to the successful rearing of these varieties, you must admit that knowing about it does make the whole operation much more exciting and eventful.

The best way to collect these spores is first to select a suitably laden frond on which the spores have started to turn brown, and wrap it in a clean sheet of white paper. Within a few days the frond will have ejected the fine powdery spores. In preparation for this, take a well-washed seed tray, and crock the entire floor with either pieces of clean clay flower pot or portions of broken brick, before filling it almost to the top with a suitable compost. Usually, I use a mixture of equal parts by volume of J.I.P. No. 1, peat and coarse sand, but you can make do with well-rotted leaf-mould instead of peat, if you wish. All this, when mixed thoroughly, should be passed through a close-mesh sieve and only the finest of the sifted mixture should be used. When using any ingredients which could possibly contain harmful microbes – such as the coarse sand and leaf-mould, for example – it is essential first to sterilise the compost, and this can be done by saturating the compost with boiling water. Only then can any germs be considered completely harmless. Leave this steaming and soggy mixture to cool before covering with a sheet of glass to exclude all harmful bacteria. A temperature of around 60°F is usually considered ideal for spore propagation although, just occasionally, some ferns like it a little warmer.

The spores can now be lightly scattered over the moist compost, and must be left as they fall, completely uncovered except for the glass lid which should be replaced. Remove the container to a suitably shaded part of the conservatory or greenhouse, and stand it in a tray which is partially filled with water. This is all that is needed to provide the perfect enclosed and humid conditions under which ferns germinate, but the compost must never be watered from the top. That would almost certainly prove fatal.

In a matter of a few weeks the green, moss-like scales should appear and a month or so later the minute fronds will rear their heads and open. Once they are well-rooted, and large enough to handle, they can be pricked out in the usual way, and repotted individually into small pots of J.I.P. No. 1. Although they must still be provided with a moist atmosphere, this must not be produced by leaving them standing in water as before, for it would certainly cause the soil to sour quickly and the roots to rot.

All the outdoor varieties must be hardened off before being transplanted into a suitable shady spot in the garden.

5. CROSS-POLLINATING AFRICAN VIOLETS

On the odd occasions when I can completely relax and indulge myself in blissful contemplation, my imaginative wanderings sometimes take me to the East Africa of nearly ninety years ago, when, on what has proved to be an historic day from the naturalist's point of view, the Baron Walter von Saint Paul-Illaire came across some African Violets (*Saintpaulia*) growing several thousand feet up in the wilds of Tanganyika (now Tanzania). These plants were eventually named after this man, who was the Governor of the province at the time, and although he never lived to see the rapidity with which their popularity grew, he must have realised the plants' potential, for he sent some of the seeds (which had been pollinated quite naturally) to Europe for cultivation.

The resulting plants probably little resembled the brilliantly coloured and varied flowering pot plants of today, because these popular specimens are the result of many years of patient cross-pollination. As I write I can see some of my own collection, many of which I originally propagated from leaf cuttings (see p. 48). They and their fellows, with all their diverse leaf shapes, flower formations and colours, have been produced over a period of years, and at the moment, the majority are carrying a number of seed pods in varying stages of development.

Once you fall in love with these free-blooming and very easily grown plants, you will naturally wish to broaden your own collection, which may comprise the more frequently seen single and semi-double white, pink, cerise, and mauve varieties to include other more unusual strains such as those with frilly-edged and double two-toned flowers, which are not so readily available. Instead of going out to buy them, you could try your hand at rearing some of the more exotic types yourself. You could even produce an entirely new strain! Although it is by no means an everyday or even every-year occurrence, it is certainly not impossible – nothing in nature is – and you stand just as good a chance of producing an original as any professional horticulturalist.

Cross-pollinating one African Violet with another – that is, transferring the pollen from one plant to another to produce a seed pod – can be achieved by using two plants of the same colour. The resulting offspring will almost always have the same colour characteristics as the parents. But things get much more interesting when you cross two flowering strains of differing colours. Imagine you have two *Saintpaulia* plants, one white, and one mauve specimen, and you want to cross them to produce plants with differently coloured heads. If this operation was as simple as mixing paints on a palette, you would expect the resulting generation to produce lilac flowers. However, colour traits in nature are not so predictable, and therefore specific hues are hard to achieve, which makes the experiment so thrilling.

When all these first generation babies have been reared to flowering maturity, by crossing one 'sister' with another, you may well obtain some very interesting colour mutations, and oddities, and quirks of nature can turn up at any time! The results of your experiments will become more and more fascinating as the successive generations are inter-crossed and reared.

It is essential when crossing one *Saintpaulia* with another, to keep a record of such a 'marriage', naming both parents. Usually the first name recorded is that of the pollen providing 'father', and the latter, that of the pollen receiving and pod-carrying 'mother'. Another pertinent point is that you should avoid leaving any of your African Violets outside so that natures' flying pollinators can get to work. If such a tragedy did occur, you could well end up with seed pods which you believe to be the results of your own handywork, when in reality the pollen came from a totally different plant, and you would never know the origins of your bastard seeds! If these seeds did happen to produce the most glorious specimen, you wouldn't know how to reproduce it, which would be nothing short of a catastrophe!

Pollination

To produce seed pods, you must first select a fading flower or two from your chosen 'father', and then transfer the yellow anthers – these are the rounded group of yellow pollen-sacs at the centre of each bloom – on to a sheet of clean paper. With a pin or fine needle, pierce each one so that the fine dust stored inside spills out. The best time for this is during a warm part of the day, and one of the simplest ways of transferring this dust is by means of a very fine brush – a moulting mascara brush which has lost most of its hairs makes a good tool for the job. However, I believe in using nature's own tools whenever possible, and so I always use the stigma from a dying flower.

Each flower has such a stigma – a fine protruding thread situated between the central pollen bags – and after removing the surrounding petals gently, you can use the tip, which looks like the antenna of a butterfly, to transfer the golden powder to the stigmas of the chosen 'mother' plant. These are a little sticky, so the dust should adhere to them without much difficulty.

The next chapter of the saga can be most frustrating, because all you can do now is watch, wait and wonder, while the green pods form, then slowly fill out and develop. The waiting will last for six to eight months before the pods finally stop growing, turn brown, and then shrivel up, like any other dried fruit! Only when this happens can the seeds inside be considered ready for plucking, and even when removed from the parent plant, they should be given a further four to six weeks in which to dry naturally. After all this waiting time, which can take as long as that needed to produce a human baby, the seeds will be ready for sowing.

6. CUTTINGS

With the great majority of both indoor and outdoor plants, it is safe to assume that cuttings will take root much more quickly, and the whole exercise will prove far easier, if you take them during the sap-flowing and growing months – that is, any time from spring to early autumn. It is generally much more difficult to induce a cutting to put down roots whilst the plant is resting during the dormant winter months but it is by no means impossible for winter cuttings to root quite successfully. Suppose that one autumn day you are offered a piece of cutting from a particularly desirable specimen. It would be foolish to decline such a gift, for it might be the only opportunity you will ever have of obtaining that particular strain. Such an eventuality is not impossible or even unlikely, because the gardening fraternity is a friendly one – it's rather like being a member of a world-wide club.

A long time ago I had such an experience which persuaded me always to accept any offerings, whatever the season, and now I have a magnificent and much-admired specimen to remind me of that chilly autumn day. Hundreds of miles from home, my husband and I stopped at an inn to rest our aching limbs and quench our thirst, when I saw a real giant of a fellow, a flowering *Begonia haageana*. This breed is often referred to as the Elephant's Ears Begonia, because of its typical large leaves which greatly resemble the flapping ears of an African elephant. It must have been about four feet high, and I was offered a stem cutting which I just couldn't have refused!

This stem cutting was severed just above a node or leaf joint so as to maintain a tidy and healthy growing plant. The wood of the stalk was very soft indeed so I wrapped it immediately in transparent polythene and hoped for the best. Unfortunately I could not spray it to prevent wilting because hairy-leaved types do not react kindly to water on their foliage. All I could do was to prevent the cutting from losing any of its own moisture contained in the leaves, by keeping it airtight.

Once back at the hotel, and armed with a suitably small pot, some J.I.P. No. 1 compost and coarse sand and a tin of hormone-rooting powder, I started to work. After trimming the stem cleanly with a sharp knife, just below a leaf joint, and removing the unwanted lower leaves, I brushed the cut end with rooting powder, and set it into a 9cm (3½in) pot containing equal portions by volume of J.I.P. No. 1 and sand. Then the pot containing barely damp compost together with the entire cutting was completely enveloped in a see-through polythene bag, which was made airtight by securing the opening with string, and finally placed in a light yet sunless siting. Although it had perforce to travel around with us for a further week or so, it did root, and is now one of the most handsome of all my specimens. And the reasons why it rooted as well as it did? Firstly, the compost was kept damp at all times, but never wet, which allowed only just enough moisture to reach the severed end. Secondly, the initial and subsequent dampenings of the surrounding air contained within the airtight polythene covering prevented the cutting from expiring moisture and consequently wilting. Another reason was the size of the pot – a point which is often overlooked – which was small enough to hold the cutting and keep the compost sufficiently warm. Also the rooting medium used, a mixture of J.I.P. No. 1 and sharp sand, was of a loose consistency in order to provide both a free flow of air and quick drainage. All of these factors are absolutely necessary for successful rooting.

Cuttings can well be rooted in practically any sort of holder – seed trays, flower pots, pans, propagating boxes, outdoor frames, even plastic yogurt cartons if you have nothing else handy – but they must be thoroughly washed and scrubbed first. It is also very important that the containers you use have ample drainage holes, and they should be well crocked with a quantity of pebbles, pieces of broken brick or fragments of clay flower pot. As I mentioned before, your rooting medium must be of a loose, porous, well aerated, and crumbly consistency, and a number of such blends are available. For instance, some people use the pre-packed J.I.P. seed compost with great success, whilst others, like myself, use a mixture of equal portions by volume of coarse sand and either J.I.P. No. 1 or peat. Some swear that setting cuttings in a blend of 5 parts of J.I.P. No. 2, 2 parts of peat, and 3 parts of sharp sand, is the absolute answer to all rooting ills. The perfect answer is probably any good mixture as long as the essential rules of propagation have been observed.

Although many plants can be reared without the provision of any artificial bottom heat, there are certain more awkward types which do need the encouragement of some additional warmth. Hardwood cuttings, for example, particularly those which are set out of doors, do take several months before they have formed roots, whilst semi- or half-ripe cuttings, when enclosed in a heated frame with a temperature of 55°–61°F (13°–16°C) will take up to four weeks. Softwood cuttings, take much more easily, and given the essential warmth and humid atmosphere of around 64°F (18°C), will root within ten to fourteen days. However, cuttings which are propagated during the winter months will naturally take somewhat longer.

Once your pieces have put down their 'feeders' it is imperative that they should be repotted into a more suitable growing compost. A sterilised and specially formulated blend such as J.I.P. Nos. 1 or 2 should be used, for these composts contain essential plant nutrients needed to promote healthy growth, unlike ordinary sand and peat mixtures which have no food value at all. Outdoor varieties which have been reared undercover must first be prepared by being gradually exposed to lower temperatures, more fresh air, and light. This is usually achieved effectively by hardening them off in a cold frame. Once the weather has become mild the hardened-off plants can be transferred individually to their permanent bed in the garden.

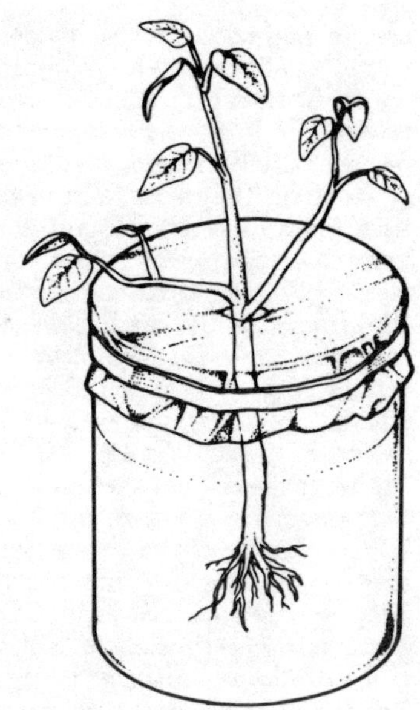

Rooting a cutting in water.

Rooting Cuttings in Water

Some of us have little luck when trying to root either stem or leaf cuttings, and often this is because, although we understand the detailed principles involved, such as how actually to take and root the chosen specimen, we cannot put into practice the art of providing just the right amount of water at the right time. This problem often foxes some of the keenest horticulturalists, with the result that the cuttings are either fed too little, causing them to shrivel and fade away, or sadly over-watered – a much more likely happening – which causes the cuttings quickly to rot and die. Now, those indoor varieties which tend to produce aerial roots (these often form at the joint of each leaf), can be induced to produce roots by sitting the cutting just above the water line of a partially filled, non-transparent container.

Cuttings severed at the leaf joints of such varieties as

the large-leaved Swiss Cheese Plant (*Monstera*), most varieties of the jungle-loving *Philodendron*, the silver and green Aluminium Plant (*Pilea*), Devils Ivy (*Scindapsus*), and many of the small-leaved and bushy peperomias, can be set on this damp seat in a warm but not hot room, whereupon they will feel the rising humidity surrounding them, and instinctively put down roots in search of moisture. Even varieties which are not inclined to produce aerial roots, for instance the free-flowering African Violet (*Saintpaulia*), the trailing Wandering Jew (*Tradescantia*), zebrinas, aquatic Umbrella Plants (*Cyperus*), and the mauve-leaved Velvet Plants (*Gynura*) can all be rooted successfully in this manner.

The reason I suggest that the cut ends stay just above the water level, rather than inserted in the water, is that those types which are more inclined to rot will stand a better chance of rooting in safety. It is extremely important to choose a container which is not transparent, because the water contained in a holder which lets in the light will soon turn stale as green algae form on the inside walls, and then cuttings never seem to root well. I usually keep a tall plastic pot specially for this purpose, but actually one of the best and most effective containers I ever owned was a black china vase, in which cuttings would produce a healthy mass of roots in a relatively short time. If you can collect and use fresh rainwater, instead of hard tap water, so much the better. To this you can add a mild dose of liquid plant fertiliser cum feed – one or maybe two drops will be ample.

To ensure that the lighter pieces, such as the soft leaf cuttings of the *Saintpaulia*, do remain above, and don't accidentally fall into the water, a safety lid made of paper or polythene should be stretched across the top of the beaker or other vessel, and tied securely. It will need a suitable number of holes corresponding approximately to the thickness of the stems, so that they can be inserted at exactly the desired level. I frequently keep cuttings like this on my sunless kitchen window-sill, for not only do they remain unharmed by the burning summer sun, but the boiling of kettles and pans of water keeps the air humid. This is first class for the cuttings, because it helps to keep the exposed top parts firm and healthy. After all, one must remember that when situated in stifling hot and dry conditions, cuttings quickly start to flag and wilt, and once this happens they will never find the strength necessary for successful rooting.

As soon as a sufficient number of roots have formed, each piece should be set into a small pot containing a suitable compost such as J.I.P. No. 1.

Softwood Cuttings

Softwood cuttings are usually taken and rooted any time from early to late summer, whilst the life-giving sap is rising freely in the still soft and juicy stems. But remember, these young and immature cuttings, because they are so sappy and moist, are inclined to lose moisture fairly quickly. So, if by any chance an unexpected visitor arrives just when you are about to set some cuttings in a suitable rooting mixture, do try to finish the job first! If this really is impossible, and you expect to be away longer than just a minute or two, always wrap the severed sections in an airtight polythene bag, or pop them into a bowl of water and cover and secure the top with polythene. This will ensure that the severed stems will not lose any moisture by transpiration during your absence, and on your return they will be so firm that they seem to be bursting with vigour and energy!

Varieties such as lupins, fuchsias, delphiniums, violas, geraniums, calceolarias, chrysanthemums and verbenas, are all propagated by softwood cuttings. Choose pieces which are firm but not hard, and cut them just below a leaf joint or node, with either a sharp knife or secateurs, on a suitable non-flowering part of the plant. The cut sections should be between 5 and 10cms long (2 to 4ins). Always remove the lower leaves on your cuttings, and after stopping any weeping or bleeding ends by brushing them with powdered charcoal, set them at a depth of one-third of their height, in a mixture of equal portions by volume of

J.I.P. No. 1, peat and sharp sand. If you prefer to, you can use the coarse sand by itself, but those who choose to do so must realise that though sand is a marvellous medium for rooting, it contains absolutely no nutrients at all. Consequently, as soon as possible after the cuttings have taken root, it is essential that they be repotted into a compost such as J.I.P. No. 1. Brushing the cut ends with a hormone-rooting powder is optional, but I do believe that using it ensures a good healthy root system, and I have found that treated cuttings do form roots noticeably quicker than others which have been left to grow unaided.

Ensure that the compost is comfortably moist but not soggy before covering the boxed or potted cuttings with polythene, tying it securely into place with string. This transparent roof will prevent moisture evaporating thus providing the close and humid conditions needed for these softwood cuttings to root.

If a bottom heat of between 60° and 64°F (16°–18°C) can be provided by a propagating frame, so much the better, and within ten days or so, maybe more depending on the variety, the cuttings should be rooting nicely. During this time they should be situated in a good yet sunless light, perhaps in a cool greenhouse or conservatory, and immediately any drops of moisture form on the inside of the polythene covering, they must be wiped away before they are able to fall on and harm the cuttings. As soon as active growth is evident, the cuttings can be repotted individually into small pots of J.I.P. No. 1.

Half-ripe and Semi-hardwood Cuttings

I suppose I can best describe a half-ripe or semi-hardwood cutting, by comparing it with the other two main types, hardwood and softwood. A half-ripe section is nothing like as old as the growth of a hardwood, neither is it as tender as the typical softwood *Pelargonium* cutting. It is really half-way between the two, and many conifers, shrubs such as camellia, *Caryopteris*, clematis, *Nerium*, and heathers are all propagated in this way. The half-ripened limb is, in fact, what its name implies – a part of the current year's growth. Only the strongest and healthiest pieces should be selected to furnish cuttings, and these can be selected either from a main bough or from any vigorous side shoot, depending on what is available.

8 to 15cm (3 to 6in) long cuttings should be taken from mid-summer to early autumn, and unless a heel cutting is required (see p. 44) the cut should be clean and straight across the member, just below a node or a leaf bud. After removing the unwanted lower leaves, dust the severed ends with a hormone-rooting powder, and plant the cuttings to a depth of between one-third and half their height. They can be set either in a cold frame or directly into the soil, as you wish, but if you use the latter method, do remember to protect them with cloches. This will also encourage them to root. Although half-ripe cuttings will obviously not root as quickly as softwood ones, I've always found that they take more quickly when set in a sandy mixture. I usually use equal portions by volume of peat and sharp sand, but if you prefer to you can use John Innes seed compost to which a small quantity of coarse sand has been added.

Ideally, such cuttings should be positioned in a light yet shaded spot, out of the sun, and on very hot days they will need at least one spraying every day. During the following spring, when the weather is suitably mild and all danger of frost has passed, you can remove all the successfully rooted ones from under the frame, and transplant them individually into your chosen part of the garden. Any which have not taken – and there are usually one or two failures – should be discarded.

Hardwood Cuttings

Taking and successfully rooting hardwood cuttings, is one of the easiest of all ways to propagate a variety of trees and shrubs, and 'hardwood' exactly describes the type of wood with which we are dealing. Cuttings are always taken from the current season's growth, when the wood is

Hardwood cuttings in a trench.

fully ripe, and usually during the dormant period from autumn to early spring. They can be anything from seven to fifteen inches in length, and varieties such as the *Cydonia*, the gooseberry, the rose, and the red and white currants are just five of numerous shrubs which can be increased in this way. Although the selected sections should be taken and set during the non-growing months, it is always as well to choose a time when the soil is still warm, and always prepare the trench on a day when the weather is reasonably mild.

If your garden soil is inclined to be too light, or too heavy, the texture must first be improved and treated, either by enriching it with some well decomposed compost and peat, or by adding some coarse sand to make it lighter and more airy. Work it in well to a depth of at least 30cms (12in). Make your V-shaped trench 12 or more cm (about 5in) deep, and dress the floor with 2.5cm (1in) of coarse sand – it will encourage the formation of the roots.

Once you have cut a number of sections, each below a leaf-joint or node, and once you have removed the unwanted lower leaves, the cuttings are ready for the bed which was prepared earlier in the day.

Set them at least half their depth, with their exposed top section leaning against the wall of the trench. Replace the soil around them and firm them down with the heel of your boot. At this time of the year it is particularly important to firm them well into position, because during the winter months, frosts are inclined to loosen and lift them. From now until the spring check them regularly and heel them in whenever it is necessary. Those of you who live in districts where the frost can be particularly severe at times may find it necessary to cover the trenched cuttings with some cloches, until the worst of the cold weather has passed.

Hardwood sections which are planted out in the open can take anything up to twelve months to root. During the next year the rooted cuttings can be lifted and moved to their permanent siting, but very small ones can be left where they are for a further twelve months.

Eye Cuttings

One comes across this form of propagation when speaking to the fortunate few who have the necessary space in a greenhouse in which to grow one or a number of grape vines. I rarely use this method, because I am usually too busy writing as well as adding to my already fair-sized collection of exotic plants and, to date, grape vines have not played a particularly important part in my plant world. Unlike my parents, for instance, who have a gorgeous and very well established black grape vine, and have on a number of occasions reared others from eye cuttings for various friends.

During the autumn or winter months a leafless portion of stem, between 3.75 and 5cm (1½ and 2in) long, and with a single 'eye', is cut out and prepared. From the stem's side opposite to this eye or bud, is sliced a thin sliver of wood and bark, no more than 3mm (⅛in) thick, from end to end of the cutting. Only by exposing this inner layer can one successfully stimulate and promote the sound rooting necessary.

This prepared section can then be potted, cut side downwards, into a mixture of moist sand and peat. It is important that the eye, which is peeping just above the compost level, should not be allowed to dry and shrivel up, and so a surrounding moist atmosphere is necessary at all times. Secure the cutting in place with pegs, and place it in a propagating box with a bottom heat of between 61°–75°F (16°–24°C).

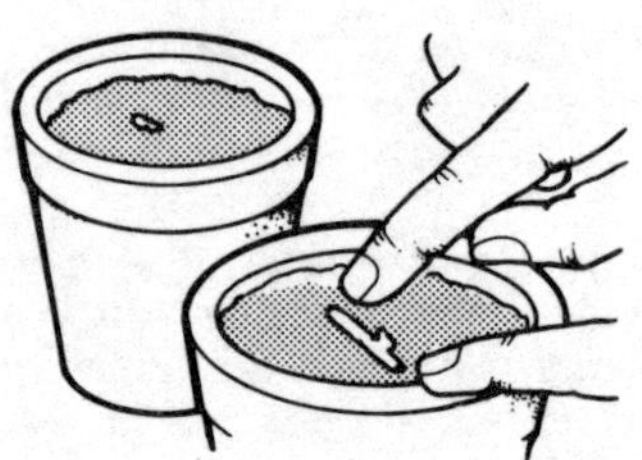

Eye cuttings. The cutting should be pushed into the soil so that only the growth bud shows.

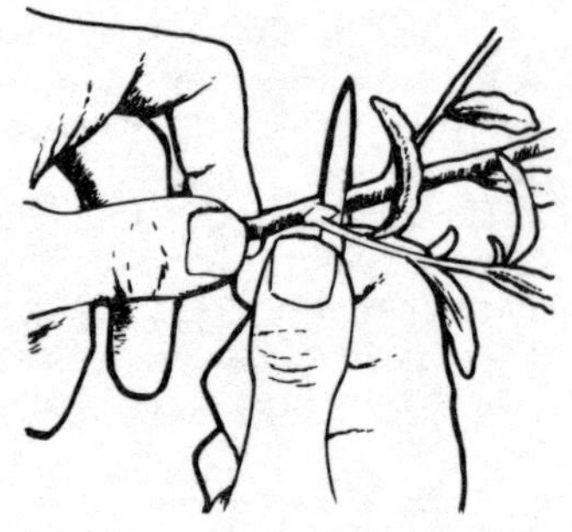

Taking a heel cutting.

Once well rooted, the eye cutting can be transplanted into a 12.5cm (5in) flower pot containing J.I.P. No. 2 compost.

Heel Cuttings

Both the hardwood and semi-hardwood varieties of shrubs and trees take longer to root than the softwooded types, but these slow-rooting ones will take much more readily when they have been propagated by heel cuttings.

A side shoot is usually selected, and a cut made between two leaf joints, or nodes. However, instead of cutting straight across the shoot, as is more usual, the cut is made at a slant, leaving attached to this severed piece a thinnish sliver of the shoot from which it is cut. This is called the heel. Once you have almost made the slanting cut, you will find that the heel part can be severed by a pull, but it is much better to cut through the attached bark as well. If the cutting is a bit ragged, it will need to be trimmed slightly with a sharp knife, before planting it in the usual way.

Propagating from Leaf Pieces

With plants such as the *Begonia rex*, a considerable number of young plants can be reared very successfully by

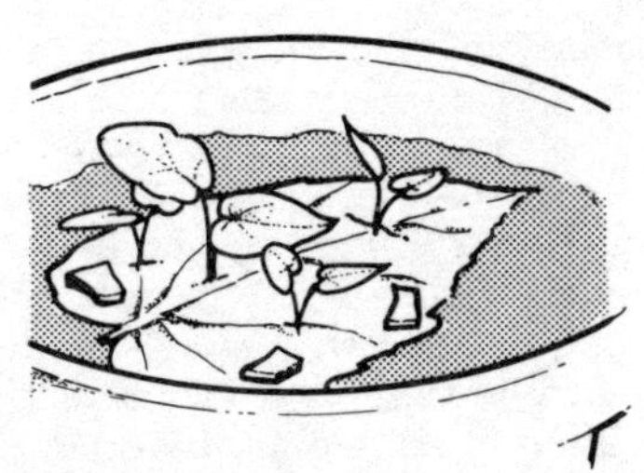

New plants growing from a begonia leaf cutting.

using a single leaf. However, the method is not the one used to root, say, the leaf of an African Violet (*Saintpaulia*), which is inserted directly into the compost. No, it is the very prominent veins on the back of the leaves, which play the active and most essential role in this type of propagation.

These veins must be encouraged to 'give birth' by nicking them at the junction with a second vein, and for this little operation you need either a sharp knife or a razor blade. Having made the nick, lay the entire leaf on its back, so that the tiny severed veins are lying absolutely flat on the compost. For the compost I always use a rooting mixture of equal parts by volume of peat and sand, which ideally should be no more than damp to the touch. The leaf must be held in close contact with the compost by means of pebbles placed strategically over the leaf surface. Cover the pot with transparent polythene, tie with raffia and after a while some small plantlets should appear. When they are well-rooted and established the polythene can be removed, and the plantlets repotted individually into a suitable compost such as J.I.P. No. 1, to which a little peat has been added.

If you don't enjoy the success you expect using this method, perhaps you would like to try an alternative one which can also be used on varieties like the *Streptocarpus* and certain strains of the *Sansevieria*. But I must emphasise now, that such cuttings taken from one *Sansevieria* in particular, namely the *S. trifasciata* 'Laurentii', will not grow true, as do the young offsets which appear above the soil, for the attractive yellow banding which is seen on many good specimens will be conspicuous by its absence. However, other strains of *Sansevieria* can be propagated very successfully in this manner, the resultant small babies being replicas of their parents. The leaves of these varieties should be cut into small squares, each portion containing a strong vein or two, and then set into compost and covered with see-through polythene as before. When the plantlets have formed and are large enough to handle safely, they should be repotted. For such attempts to be successful, it is important always to keep cuttings well out of the sun, particularly during the summer months, otherwise scorching and shrivelling of the leaves will almost certainly occur. Although this method can succeed at almost any time of the year, it really is best to stick to the growing months, when the adult plants are strong and healthy. They are usually at their peak during the summer.

Leaf Cuttings

Apart from the normal pleasures accorded to loyal and avid gardeners during the summer months, – such as the once dead-looking winter borders now ablaze with multicoloured annuals and perennials, the boughs of the well-cared-for fruit trees heavily laden with blossom, and the charming flowering shrubs and climbers, all bearing a colourful display of large and gloriously-tinted blooms, – one of my main delights during these sap-rising months is in the rearing of various plants from leaf-cuttings.

Old favourites like *Saintpaulia*, *Gloxinia*, *Peperomia*, *Streptocarpus*, and *Begonia* are all good subjects when taken with a section of stalk attached, but choosing the right sort of leaf is especially important. When you have the growing plant in front of you, and you are considering which of the many leaves to use, remember that you are really selecting the parent of your future young plants. Consequently, you should reject the fairly old and dark-coloured lower foliage, for the leaves are coming to the end of their lives, and don't really have the necessary vigour to

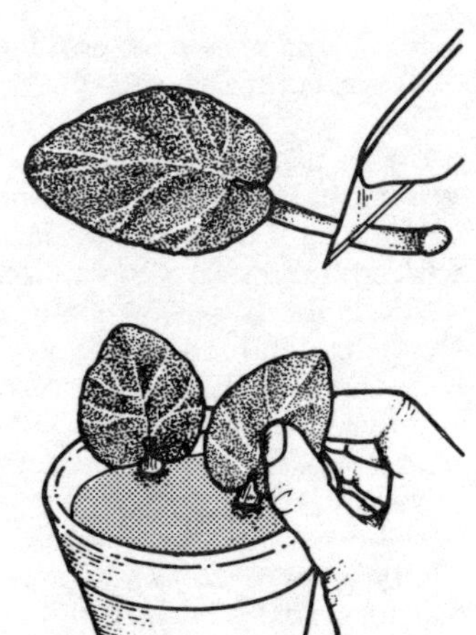

Leaf cuttings from a saintpaulia.

produce strong new plantlets. Neither are the very fresh and pale new leaves nearer the centre or the top much better – they are too young. No, the perfect choice is the neither young nor old leaf of middling colour density, which appears firm, well-shaped and strong.

The stalk should be cut close to the main stem, even if it is too long for your purpose. Never leave any untidy and protruding pieces behind because more than likely they will rot and cause real problems to the once healthy specimen. Once you have cut the stalk cleanly with a sharp knife, trim it to the desired length, dust the end with a hormone-rooting powder, and set it at an angle of about 40° or 45° in a rooting medium such as sharp sand or a mixture consisting of half sand and half peat. I never believe it's a good idea to plant the stem too deeply, because it makes rotting more likely, so just bury it deep enough comfortably to support the leaf. At no time should the compost be wetter than damp, and if there is no propagating box available, to provide the cuttings with a bottom heat of around 60° to 64°F, then cover the individual pots with transparent polythene secured with string. Then keep the cuttings in a light yet sunless room which is warm, but never hot. Once new shoots have formed, and grown several leaves apiece, they should each be repotted into 7.5cm (3in) pots of J.I.P. No. 1.

Saintpaulia leaf cuttings
When dealing with *Saintpaulia* cuttings, the stem of the cutting may be split once or twice lengthwise, a practice which often results in one leaf producing not just one, but several plantlets at a time. Another fascinating point is that the characteristics of the future *Saintpaulia* can sometimes be partially determined by how the stem is cut. For instance, if the leaf has a section of stem attached, the resulting plant will be more inclined to resemble its parent. If, however, a leaf with no stem is successfully propagated to adulthood, the new plant is much more likely to have traits which differ from those of its immediate forebears. Then you may have a strain which has different shaped foliage or flowers, and different colours and tones as well. If any such freaks can be reproduced exactly a second time, by rearing further plants from leaf-cuttings, then they are called sports, unlike other oddities called mutations which can only be reproduced a second time by seed.

Leaf-bud Cuttings

This method of propagation is usually practised with camellias at the height of the growing season. A leaf bud is selected and sliced downwards, so that the entire bud, the leaf and some of the bark from the parent stem all come away together. Paring a bud with a leaf attached is necessary, because it is the leaf's function to convey the nutriment which will encourage the formation and development of the new roots.

Dust the newly severed end with a hormone-rooting powder, before firmly planting it in a moist and sandy mixture. All that should remain exposed is the leaf. Spray this greenery frequently but lightly with water, but never let the soil itself become any wetter than damp. Provide a bottom heat of between 16° and 18°C (61°–64°F).

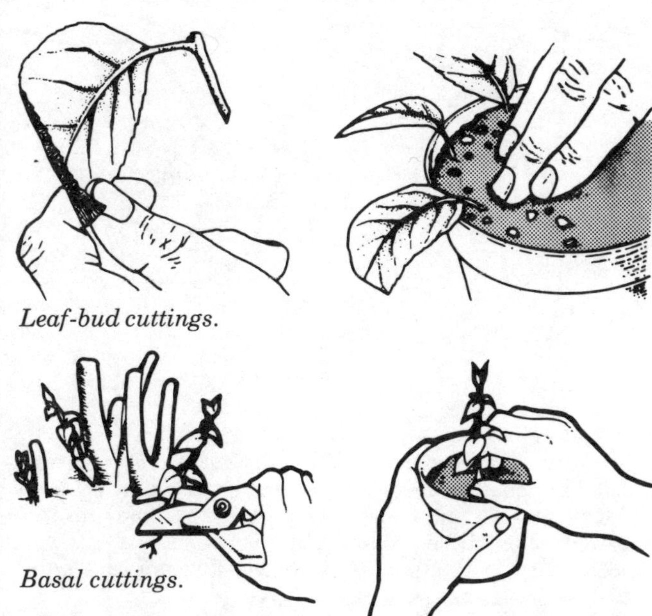

Leaf-bud cuttings.

Basal cuttings.

Basal Cuttings

This method of propagation is most commonly used when rearing chrysanthemums and dahlias, and it involves severing a young and non-flowering shoot, either at the base of the plant or just below the soil surface. The cut must be made tidily, with a sharp knife, and the severed end dusted with a hormone-rooting powder. Either set it in a pot containing a suitably open and sandy-textured mixture, and cover with a cloche, or plant it directly into a shaded cold frame.

Both the cutting and the surrounding atmosphere need to be kept moist, with a daily overhead light misting, particularly during the warmer summer months. When the cutting has rooted and has started to make some visible growth, it can be planted out-of-doors without any overhead protection.

Thick root cuttings. Cuttings from plants with fine roots should be laid on top of the soil.

Root Cuttings

It is such a pity, and a waste too, that more gardeners don't take root cuttings as a means of propagating their existing stock. Plants resulting from this method are often stronger than those produced by other forms of cuttings, and frequently the blooms are better and larger. This is why root cuttings are usually considered to be more reliable, and far superior to, say, leaf cuttings. The method is very simple, has a high success rate, and yet one rarely sees it practised.

In my grandfather's day – which was really not very long ago – he would lift certain varieties during the dormant season from autumn to early spring, and take cuttings. I remember a clump of mint and some seakale which came under the knife one year, and possibly so did all sorts of charming flowering types such as the blue-flowering *Anchusa italica*, the *Catananche* and *Verbascum*, the perennial white-flowering *Gypsophila paniculata*, the hollyhock, and the *Romneya*, with their fragrant heads of white. You can add the unmistakable and almost tubular-headed *Acanthus*, the *Echinops*, which has thistle-like blue faces, the metallic-like headed *Eryngium*, and the glorious flowering *Papaver orientale*, in its various hues of red, pink, or orange. All of these, and more besides, can be increased using this easy technique. Although it is not essential completely to uproot the plant which you wish to propagate, the task of selecting and severing the best pieces of root is thereby made much simpler.

Just as it is important to choose the right leaf or stem cutting for propagation, so, and for exactly the same reasons, should only the plumpest, thickest, and strongest-looking roots be selected. The healthy and well-fed look you want still applies to the finer-rooted types such as mint. Make a clean cut straight across nearest the root stock, and trim the thinner and tapering tail end at a slanting angle.

If your 5 to 7.5cm (2 to 3in) root cutting is taken from one of the fine, fibrous rooted specimens, like *Phlox* or *Primula*, lay it on the top of your prepared rooting mixture. Then sprinkle a fine layer of compost just to cover it. Other thicker types should, however, be set, slanting cut downwards, so that the straight top is just below the soil level. Your prepared box, pot or pan (depending on how many pieces you intend to grow) must have some drainage holes, and these will need to be covered with a layer of crocks. Then you may add your compost, perhaps a mixture of J.I.P. No. 1, peat or leafmould, or an equal quantity by volume of peat and coarse sand. Keep the compost moist and warm to promote root development, which I usually ensure by covering it with a sheet of clear glass. After the shoots and buds have developed each root cutting can be planted out individually, into any suitable garden border.

Piping

Taking and rooting piping cuttings is the easiest way to propagate a number of carnations and pinks, for all you have to do is grip a young and non-flowering tip shoot between your finger and thumb, just above a leaf joint. Give it a quick sharp jerk, and it will come away easily and cleanly.

A piping does not need to be trimmed at all, but the pale green pulled end should be dusted with rooting powder, before you set it into a pot of sandy compost.

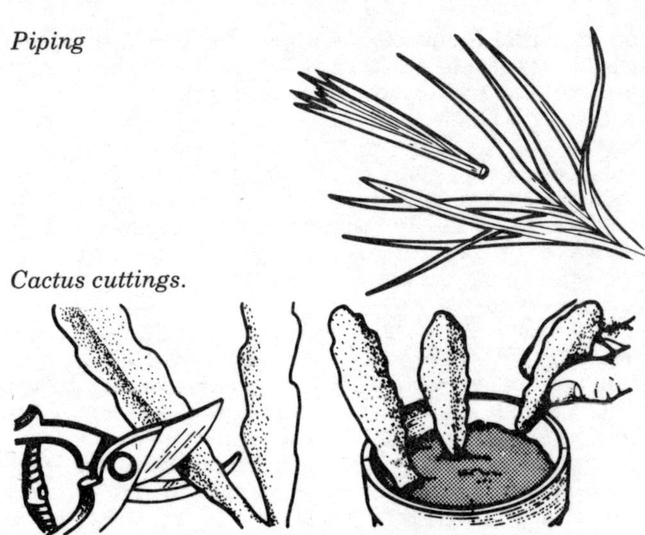

Piping

Cactus cuttings.

Cactus and Succulent Cuttings

Some time ago, one of my succulents, the rosette-shaped *Byrnesia weinbergii*, fell off the back of the greenhouse staging on to the gravel trays below. For several weeks this mishap went completely unnoticed because at the time the entire surface was crammed full of many other cacti and succulent cuttings and plants. And by the time the fallen fellow was retrieved, it was certainly doing very nicely without my help, because some of its pale and greyish 'leaves' had broken off and become rooted on the damp gravel surface. The result amounted to more than half a dozen ready-rooted leaf cuttings. These up and coming plants were set individually into small well-crocked pots, containing 2 parts of J.I.P. No. 2, 1 part of peat, and 1 part of coarse sand, on to which mixture was sprinkled a little bone meal.

After they had fallen, the cut ends had calloused over quite naturally, in much the same way as they would when growing in the wild, and not only this particular breed, but others too, such as the *Sedum*, *Crassula*, *Echeveria*, *Pachyphytum*, *Graptopetalum* and even the more leafy-looking *Gasteria* and *Haworthia* can all be propagated quite easily in the same way. However, when taking any kind of cactus or succulent cutting, it is most important to remember that the severed sections should always be allowed to dry and 'heel over' in a warm yet shaded room, before setting them in a suitable compost. If this rule is not strictly adhered to, the majority will rot, even before they have the opportunity to put down roots.

Dusting the cut ends with a hormone-rooting powder, though not absolutely essential, can speed up the whole process, particularly when dealing with some slow-growing types. Alternatively, the open cut can be treated either with a dusting of flower of sulphur or charcoal, which will protect it from decay.

There are several eminently suitable rooting composts on the market, such as vermiculite or perlite, which are considered extremely good, but if you want to mix your own, a worthwhile blend is one of equal portions, by volume, of coarse sand and peat. When rearing this type of cutting, I usually keep to my own rule of moistening the barely damp compost only when the cuttings have rooted and sent up perfect miniature replicas of the parent plant. You can spray them very lightly just once.

Although cactus and succulent pieces are best reared during the growing months, that is from spring to autumn, an accident occuring to one of your specimens during the depths of winter, which causes it to die, should not deter you from taking cuttings. If such a thing does happen during the dormant months, do try to provide the cuttings with some bottom heat. On one such occasion, when my propagating box was filled to bursting point, I successfully reared some succulent sections by inserting the already dried and severed ends in a completely dry and sandy soil. I covered the top of the pot securely with transparent polythene, and set it on a wide shelf just above a small radiator, to give it the necessary bottom warmth. The pot was positioned close to the wall, so that the cuttings were not harmed by the rising hot air.

During the non-growing winter months, many over-watered cacti and succulents soon come to a pappy and pulpy end. If any of your specimens start to take on the visual signs of root-rot, don't hesitate to take and root any healthy cuttings as quickly as you can. For instance, the jointed pads of varieties such as the *Opuntia* and the *Zygocactus* can easily be detached and rooted as leaf cuttings, whilst the tall and columnar *Cereus*, the branching tree-like *Euphorbia*, the *Rhipsalis* and the *Epiphyllum* can all be severed cleanly a little way from the top with a sharp razor blade or fine-edged knife. Never use a cutting tool with a serrated or toothed blade, because this will hack the specimen in a jagged fashion, instead of making a tidy and clean-edged cut. Allow the severed ends to dry and callous over before dusting them with a branded hormone powder such as Seradix. Then set them in a damp rooting compound, keeping it no wetter than moist at any time. Only after they show signs of having taken should they be repotted into small pots, which should contain a good layer of broken brick, and a suitable compost such as the one I mentioned earlier. There again, one can use a specially blended and pre-packed cactus compost, but if you really prefer to mix your own, use equal portions, by volume, of sterilised loam or J.I.P. No. 2 and coarse sand to which a little crushed brick has been added. If you want a slightly richer recipe, an equal portion of well-rotted leaf-mould can also be added.

7. BUDDING

Gardeners who are enthusiastic rose growers will be especially interested in the practice of budding. Basically, it is a form of propagation which one could describe as both aiding and speeding up the natural course of events.

The object of the exercise is to improve the growth of certain varieties which find it difficult to develop and produce flowers en masse because their root system is not as strong or as extensive as it should be. So we help them along by transplanting growth buds – which must not be mistaken for flower buds – into the stock of a chosen sturdy and robust variety, such as the *Rosa manetti*, the *R. polyantha simplex*, the *R. canina*, the *R. laxa* or one of the many strains of *R. rugosa*.

Budding is usually attempted when the sap is rising, at the height of the growing season, normally from early until late summer. A healthy and well-developed leaf bud, from the current year's growth of your selected rose bush, should be removed with a budding knife, together with a sliver of wood and bark to which the bud is attached, rather like removing a piece of orange peel with a knife. This operation should preferably be performed at the moment you wish to marry the two sections together, because the bud will start to dry immediately the cut is complete. However, if need be, moisture at the cut can be conserved by wrapping the bud in moist sphagnum moss until you are able to complete the job.

You must make a T-shaped cut in the bark of your stock at ground level for bush roses, and 1.25 to 1.5m (4 to 5ft) above ground for standard roses. The incision must be just deep enough to take and house the bud, whilst the top, horizontal part of it must be about 1cm (½in) long, and the vertical downward part nearer to 3.75cm (1½in). Now, using the blunt end of the knife, gently ease open the bark

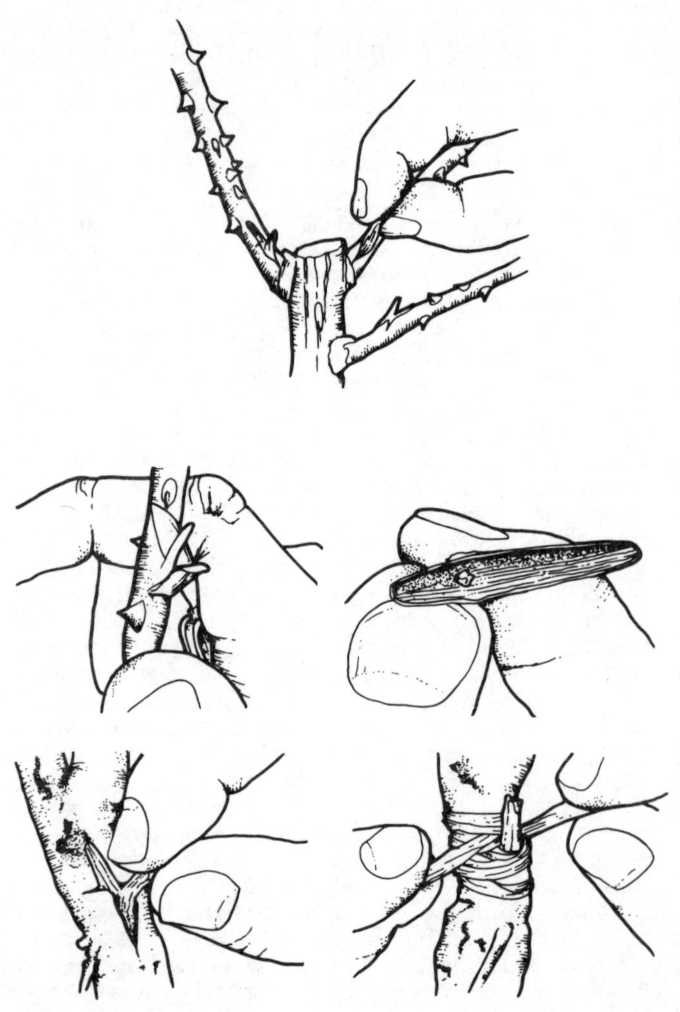

Budding.

so that you are able to slide the freshly severed bud into place. The bud must lie flat and close, to enable it to mould itself to the inner wooded section of the stock. Then bandage the entire wound with raffia in a criss-cross fashion, so that all but the exposed bud-head is bound firmly but not very tightly together.

It will take several weeks before you really know whether the budding experiment has been a success or failure. If the bud has not merged and united with the stock, it will sooner or later begin to wilt and die, but signs of success will be visible when the bud starts to plump out and grow. Only then can the raffia be cut at the back of the binding to allow a free flow of sap to the newly implanted bud. In the following spring, the stock must be pruned back to within an inch of the budding, and any suckers which appear from the roots should be cut right back.

8. GRAFTING

The technique of grafting was certainly known in Roman times, and some authorities believe that the oldest and most knowledgeable of all gardening nations, the Chinese, practised this form of propagation many thousands of years ago.

The basic principle of grafting is somewhat similar to the onc involved in budding, except that instead of transplanting one or several single growth buds into the stem (stock) of a well-rooted shrub or tree, an entire section of wood is concerned. This woody cutting is called the scion. The reason for doing this is quite simple. Some plants, shrubs and cacti in particular, are often very beautiful to look at, yet only possess a relatively small and inefficient root system. Then there are others which, though uninteresting and plain, have a wonderfully strong and vigorous root growth. So, by combining the best traits of both by simple surgery, the resultant specimen will grow more quickly and flower more freely.

Two things are necessary for the operation. The scion and stock must be healthy, and both plants must be at the peak of their growing season. Then it is that the two sections of the grafted plant have a far better chance of readily marrying and knitting together.

I believe that there are about forty different methods of grafting, some of which are now seldom if ever used, and later we will be discussing quite a few of the more commonly practised ones in detail. Meanwhile, let's first talk about the basic construction of a shrub or tree; this is necessary because success could well depend on your having such an understanding, whilst failure might be because you were unaware of what should be going on unseen, below the graft.

When you cut through a branch or stem, you will see

that there is the protective outer coating of skin or bark, and the centre part, which is somewhat pithy and woody. Contained between these two is the vital layer of green plant cells called cambium which, when given the opportunity, will unite with similar cells. The important part of grafting is successfully to connect the cambium of the cut scion with the cells contained in the stock, so that they will knit together, thus joining two separate entities into one whole plant. If the two sections are not 'married' exactly, cambium to cambium, and then bound firmly together, they cannot grow into one.

Only two tools are essential for this job; a very sharp blade such as a budding knife and plenty of raffia to bandage the stock and scion together. Before we go any further it is imperative both to realise the need for, and to practise, absolute cleanliness, and so, after every operation, your knife must be cleaned well in preparation for next time. Grafting two specimens together is very like performing a human transplant, for in a similar way, scion and stock can only be made to join together if they are both compatible in the first instance. Fortunately, it is far less complicated with plants, because this compatibility is normally found in specimens belonging to the same genus.

Although grafting is practised at the end of the dormant season, when the sap is rising in early spring, a number of scions can be cut and prepared a month or so beforehand, in late winter. Always pass over the weak and puny branches for those one-year-old shoots which look wonderfully strong and healthy. Each scion must have at least three growth buds which should not have started to burst, and should be firm and well-developed. Cut preferably a few more lengths than you might need, tie and label them together, and then bury them in the garden. The perfect spot is a cold, unsheltered area near a wall or fence, where the scions will stay cool and the buds will not be encouraged to burst open before the operation is completed. A couple of months or so later, when they are needed, the scions should be dug up and washed thoroughly so that they are clean and free from any gritty bits, which,

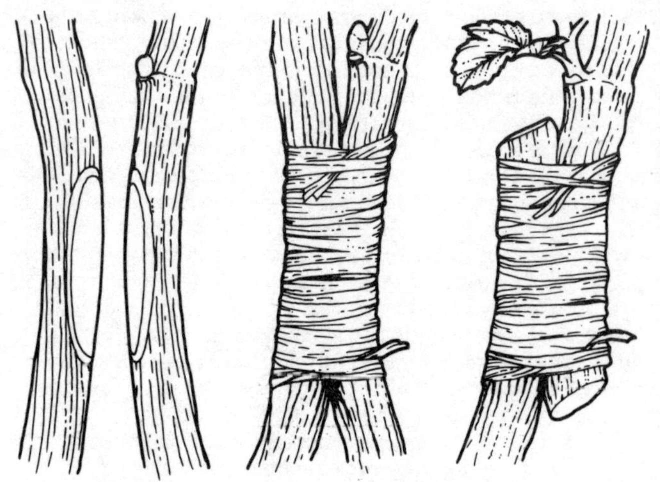

Approach grafting.

however small, could easily impede the perfect marriage of the two sections. Always choose the very firm part of the cutting, and with a sharp knife cut it to within three buds. Depending on the variety, each piece will probably be between 10 and 15cm (4 and 6in) long.

Once your graft is completed, bind the two sections firmly together with raffia, or if you prefer it, you can secure and seal the wound with grafting wax, or specially manufactured plastic tape.

Here are a number of fully described grafting methods.

Approach or Inarching Grafting

This method, as one would imagine from its name, involves uniting the scion and the stock, face to face, whilst both the stock and the entire scion are still supported by their own individual root systems. Certain varieties such as vines, some citrus trees, and the beautiful flowering magnolias and camellias are grafted in this fashion. For this method to work, the two plants must be fairly close together, so that a section of bark and wood can be cut away from the two opposite branches, to expose the green cambium layers below. The branches are then held, cut to cut, and firmly bandaged together.

After about eight weeks, when the union has knitted together nicely, the upper parts of the stock should be partially severed just above the binding, and the lower part of the scion partially severed at the bottom of the binding. After a further four or five weeks, the severing may be completed leaving the two specimens to grow independently.

Bench Grafting

Bench grafting is not really a true grafting technique at all. As its name implies, it is grafting not out-of-doors, but inside, on the greenhouse or conservatory bench. This is most commonly practised in parts of the world where the winter weather is particularly severe, as it ensures the stock is protected and housed under cover during the spring.

Under such encouraging warm conditions, the stock slowly awakens and this is the time for tongue-grafting the scion and stock. Afterwards the joined specimens are left exactly where they are for just a week or so, before being hardened off outside in a cold frame.

Bridge Grafting

This is an absolutely marvellous technique, used not so much in the field of propagating, but as a means of improving good trees which have perhaps been accidentally damaged or become diseased. Take my tip and learn this by heart, so that you can do the operation blindfolded if you have to!

It involves the bridging together of two healthy and undamaged portions of the tree, by using scions taken

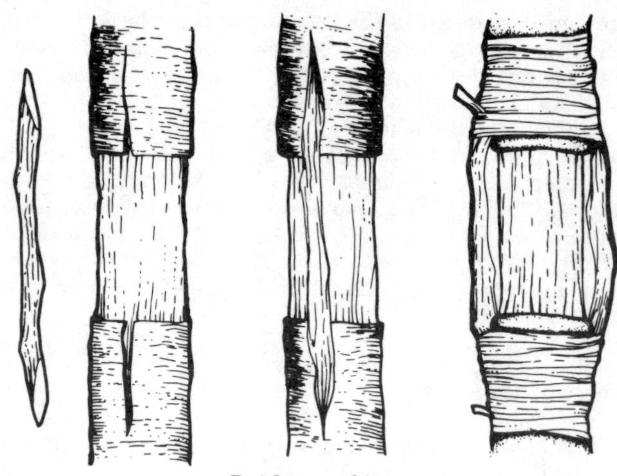

Bridge grafting.

from another tree of the same variety. Suppose that you have a favourite specimen, parts of which have canker. The unwanted and unsightly sections must first be stripped of bark, right back to a healthy portion of the branch or trunk. The bark must be cut away tidily with a sharp knife. Then make a vertical incision, about 3–5cm ($1\frac{1}{2}$–2in) long, in both the healthy upper and lower remaining sections of the bark. Bridge these two parts together by inserting a couple of scions, one each side of the gap, first cutting both ends of the scions at an angle. These ends should then be placed together cut to cut, so that the two exposed layers of cambium merge together. Bind into place with raffia and seal with wax.

Awl Grafting

The dictionary describes an awl as being 'a small pricking tool', which probably explains why this particular type of graft was given its name. An awl graft is performed by making a small incision in the bark with a small sharp knife, at a point in the stock where there are no shoots at all. This cut bark, or outer skin, is lifted so that a sliver of scion can be inserted. Then the whole is bound together and treated in the usual way.

Framework Grafting

This particular technique involves the framing of an existing, poor fruiting tree with many new scions from another variety. In this case, all the side shoots of the tree are first cut right back, whilst the main branches are retained and used for grafting a number of scions. Each scion must have between six and eight growth buds apiece, and once they are grafted on to the boughs, will produce the much-needed fruiting shoots.

There are several different means of achieving this desirable end, and so we will deal with them individually and in alphabetical order.

Bark Grafting

This method may at first sound awkward, but don't let that deter you, because it's really quite simple. Firstly, you have to prepare the base of the scion which you are to insert into the bark by cutting it so that the right-hand side has a long slanting cut, and the remaining left side a shorter less sharply angled one. In other words, when it is ready to insert, it will look like a very much lop-sided wedge. Next make an incision in the bark of the tree, in the middle of a bough. It's not always very easy to explain this in words, but this cut must be L-shaped, but upside down, or like a number 7 made the right way up.

With your knife, gently raise the outer skin of the bark, and insert the scion so that the longer sided wedge is facing to the right, and the shorter wedge to the left. Finally secure the two in place by either hammering a small nail through both the scion and stock, or by using a gimp pin, finishing off by sealing it with either tape or grafting wax.

Oblique Side-grafting

This method of grafting is usually performed on a section

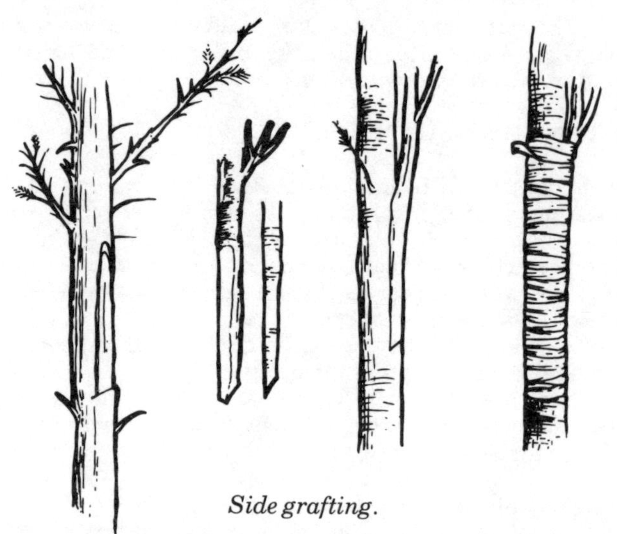
Side grafting.

of branch which has few or no shoots, at a spot where some new and fruiting laterals are required, but it can be used at any point where new growth is required.

The scion should have an inch-long, pointed wedge – almost like a well-sharpened pencil – with at least six healthy buds. Make a 5cm (2in) circular or oval cut, at the desired position and angle in one of the main stems. Raise the 'tongue' of the bark and insert the wedge of the scion. The bark will automatically hold this newcomer in place, However, it should still be taped or waxed in the usual way, to keep it rain-water proof.

Side Grafting

This form of propagation is often used when dealing with such varieties as conifers. Prepare the end of your scion by whittling it to an uneven point, then make an incision in the bark of a leading branch of the parent-to-be. The cut should be at a slanting angle of about 20°. Then after introducing the wedged part of the scion, cover the entire opening, in the manner described previously.

Stub Grafting

This method of propagation differs from the other methods used in frameworking. Instead of cutting into one of the leading branches, this graft uses one of the strong, but secondary boughs – that is one which is growing from a major branch.

Prepare the tip of your scion, as always, in a wedge shape, one side of the wedge being somewhat longer, and consequently the angle more acute, than the other. Make the cut in the bark of the lateral shoot just deep enough to take the prepared end of the scion. If the cut can be made at the junction, then so much the better, but it must be made as close as possible to the adjoining major bough. Now bend the minor bough back, so as to open the cut just sufficiently to insert the scion, the shorter side facing downwards. Once in place, the minor bough can be released, whereupon it will shoot back to grip the scion tightly. Although I've heard of some gardeners who don't always bind this type of graft, I prefer to, because it keeps out the air and prevents the graft from drying out.

Crown or Rind Grafting

This is often practised on very old fruit trees which are failing to produce the crop they once did. Grafting a couple of scions under the bark of each of the main branches gives them a rekindled fruiting life. This type of grafting can be carried out on the largest of trees, and, as always, it involves having your prepared scions ready to hand.

They can either be suitable strong budded shoots left over from the pruning, or scions cut from another tree of exactly the same variety. The end of each must first be cut into a 2.5cm (1in) long wedge, and one essential is that every scion must have a growth bud situated immediately above the V-shaped tip. First trim back all the branches of the tree like a crown – hence the name. Then make two vertical incisions in the bark of the opposing sides of each branch, close to the point of severance. Lift back the bark, and slide a pointed scion into each cut, so that the green

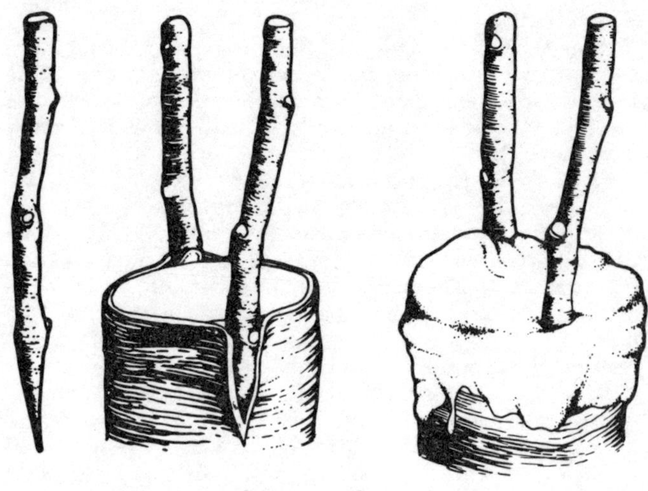

Crown grafting.

cambium layers of both the stock and scions are resting snugly against each other. The bud situated just above the cut tip of each scion must be left exposed on exactly the same level as the newly pruned branches. Then tape and seal in the usual way.

Saddle Grafting

I imagine that to even the uninitiated gardener this method of grafting is the best known of all. Indeed, I can remember very clearly, grafting some of my parents' rhododendrons in this way, when I was still a small child of nine or ten. It really is a marvellous means of increasing this often deliciously fragrant and very lovely flowering shrub. However, the 'saddle' can be used on all sorts of plants including fruit trees, but it is important that both the scion and stock are of approximately the same thickness.

The process does not involve the insertion of the scion

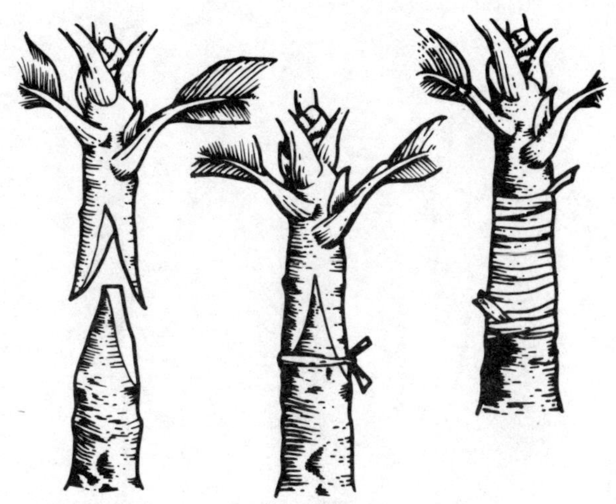

Saddle grafting.

beneath the bark, as in previous grafting techniques I have described, but in whittling and merging the scion and stock into one. First check the chosen scion to make sure that it has at least one growth bud attached, then whittle the base into an inverted V-shaped 'saddle'. Once the stock has been severed a short distance above the soil, the top portion must be shaped into a wedge so that the scion can sit cosily on top of the stock. That done, bind the graft with raffia in the usual way.

Splice Grafting

Many people perform this splice grafting several times a year, yet, when you come to talk to them about grafting generally, they seem quite perplexed, believing it to be some alien, technical job. Some just don't seem to associate what they have been doing quite naturally with what they understand as an advanced skill.

My own husband was one such person! Apparently,

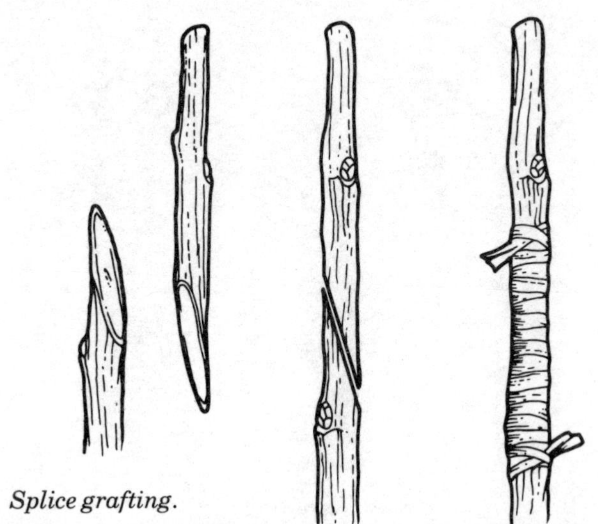

Splice grafting.

many years before I ever knew him, he accidentally snipped off one of the leading flowering stems from his clematis, whilst attempting to cut back some other shrubs nearby. His only hope lay in binding the two snipped ends together, as one would with a splice graft, and apparently it worked extremely well! The only difference was that his scion was the taller and topped clematis shoot.

Apart from clematis, other varieties such as the rose and the broom, can be spliced and grafted together. Don't make a straight cut, but sever the two pieces, the rooted stock and the shorter budded scion, at an angle. Only then can they be suitably fitted and bound together in the usual way.

Top Working

Top working is not unlike framework grafting in principle, and tired trees can be completely rejuvenated in the shortest possible time. All but a couple of the leading branches should be pruned back hard, to within about 1 metre (3ft) of the trunk. The reason for leaving these two untrimmed ones out of the proceedings is that they will serve a very useful purpose by inducing the sap to rise, and this is exactly what is needed for the scions and stock to unite.

The scions are grafted on to each of the severed boughs, and bound and sealed in exactly the way described in crown or rind grafting (see p. 65). After a couple of years have elapsed, when the scions have become an integral part of the tree, the two still untouched boughs can be pruned and grafted in the same fashion.

Wedge or Cleft Grafting

It is some considerable time since I last saw wedge or cleft grafting practised and it just may be that, like so many other skills nowadays, it is fast becoming almost defunct. Despite this, however, it is still considered an extremely useful and effective means of grafting scions on to any fairly large and thick-limbed tree.

To try it, you will first have to get out your axe or some similar splitting tool, because you will need to make a cleft or split in the top of a sawn-off branch. This split must then be prized and kept open with the aid of a strong tool such as a large chisel, whilst two scions, one at either side, are inserted in the split. These scions, with several growth buds attached to each one, must be about 10cm (4in) long, with a cut wedge-shaped end. As in all instances of grafting, it is the layer of green cells, known as cambium, which does the necessary joining work, and so the cambium contained in both the cut scion and the split stock, must be closely positioned together.

After removing the chisel or other prizing tool, bind the split and scions with raffia or tape, fill in the central split with clay, and finally seal the whole area with grafting wax.

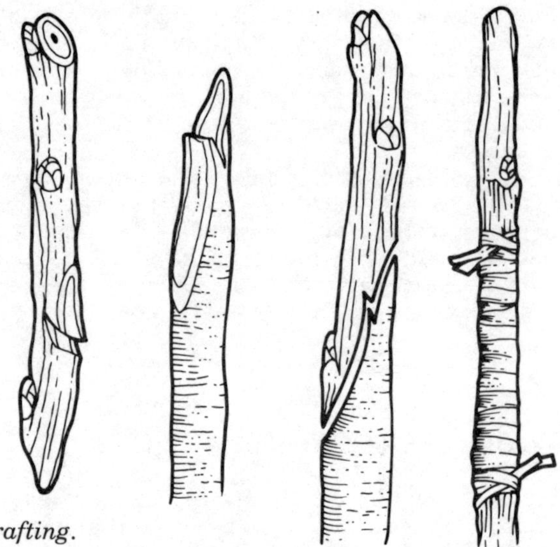

Whip grafting.

Whip or Tongue Grafting

This type of graft is frequently performed on young ornamental and fruit trees, and for it to be successful, both the scion and stock must be of approximately the same thickness. The principle involves making a tongue in both the scion and stock, so that they will fit together perfectly like a jigsaw puzzle.

The budded scion must first be prepared by cutting one end, not straight across, but at a longish gradual slant, the length of which should measure between 3.75 and 5cm (1½ and 2in). Into the centre of this gradual slant must be cut a notch (see illustration). After being pruned to within a few inches of the ground, the chosen root stock must also be cut in the same slanting and notched way, so that the two, when pieced together, will fit perfectly. Join the scion on to the stock, taking care with the fitting, bind together with moistened raffia and seal with grafting wax.

Grafting Cacti

The three most frequently used methods are cleft, flat and whip grafting, and the success of the first is very much dependent on whether the two cuts fit snugly together. The incision to be made in the stock (the rooted bottom section) must be at the height to which you wish to reduce and remodel your cactus.

Make a clean V-shaped cut in the top of the stock, using a small and very sharp knife, and then, having cut the bottom of the scion into a wedge-shape of the same size, insert the scion in the stock. The V and the wedge shapes must be cut so that one fits snugly into the other.

Flat grafting is practically self-explanatory, but this practice can only be successful if both the scion and stock are approximately the same width. Cut straight across first the stock, and then the scion, and place the lopped latter section on top of the rooted stock. Secure both in position with raffia.

Whip or tongue grafting looks very much like a one-sided version of the cleft design, but in reverse. Once you have sliced the top of the stock straight across, instead of making a V-shaped incision, you make a single slanting cut from the centre of the first and flat-topped incision, outwards towards the side, at an angle of about 45°. The scion is also cut at the same angle to fit the stock.

Once the scion is in position, the two can be fastened and held together with a long cactus spine, and then bound with raffia. Newly-grafted specimens should be fed occasionally and watered in much the same way as any other ordinary healthy cactus, but care must be taken that no moisture is allowed to fall on to or penetrate the wound. For the first ten days or so, the patients will benefit from a warm, airy, yet sunless position, and once the cut is completely healed, the raffia can be removed.

9. DIVISION

I rarely think of division solely as a means of vegetative propagation, but rather as an insurance against ills such as disease, and poor, sickly and dying growth. When mature and thick-rooted masses of Michaelmas daisies, lupins, and montbretias are multiplying year after year, and consequently stretching out in seach of more space, certain problems are bound to arise. The overgrown and tightly-packed clumps will in time become weakened in the struggle, with the result that a once large and healthy plant will give up the fight and die. The remaining few sickly sections will be vulnerable to all sorts of pests and diseases. One of the aims of gardening is to ensure that vigorous, free-flowering plants continue to grow and bloom in profusion, so why not foster and spread our things of beauty by splitting clumps of some years' standing, into smaller sections?

Division is also an extremely simple, useful and effective means of propagation, the resultant pieces always growing true to type. Tackling the task is a nice little standby job to keep you warm and active in the garden during the dormant winter months, when there is little else to do.

Dividing Fibrous-rooting Varieties

Plants such as the *helianthus*, the upright *solidago* (Golden Rod), with 'torches' of pure gold, the familiar Michaelmas daisy, the yellow, red, bronze and gold flowering *helenium*, the *rudbeckia* (Cone Plant), which has long-lasting, cone-shaped flowers, the *phlox*, and the *chrysanthemum maximum* (Shasta daisy), recognised by its typical yellow-eyed daisy-like heads of white, can all be divided quite easily.

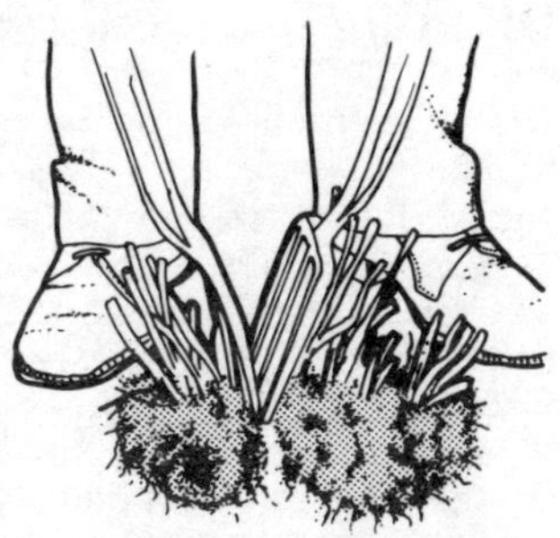

Division of a thick, fibrous-rooting clump, using two forks.

After digging up your plants and shaking off much of the soil, you can gently tease them apart with your hands. However, there are always some more difficult and deeply-matted clumps which need the help of a small trowel or hand-fork. If this treatment won't budge them, then two gardening forks will surely do the trick. Each fork should be driven right into the heart of the clump, so that both are close together and back to back. Then, with one hand on each handle, you can prize them apart. Those centre sections which look even slightly old, woody, and run-down, should be discarded in favour of the younger and more vital outer pieces, each of which should have several buds and shoots attached. Replant each such piece in the usual way.

Dividing Varieties with Hard, Woody Crowns

These types include the everyday and well-known delphiniums and lupins, which are best split up at the beginning of spring. The roots must be shaken free of all soil and then washed in luke-warm water, otherwise it would be impossible to see the very important buds clearly. These are vital, because every divided piece must have a portion of root and a bud or two attached or it cannot be replanted. Use a very sharp knife to sever the pieces cleanly.

Dividing Rhizomatous-rooting Types

A rhizomatous plant is one with a creeping, almost tuber-like underground stem, which serves as a sort of pantry for storing essential nutrients. The 'pantries' can vary enormously in size, some of the various forms of iris having quite thick ones, whilst others of such as the lily-of-the-valley are fairly fine. These rhizomes, when cut into 7.5cm (3in) lengths, can be nurtured and reared into separate plants. The inner part, that is the very heart of the specimen, should never be used because it is frequently diseased and often far too old. Only the younger rhizomes on the outer flanks should be cut cleanly into pieces, each containing some young and strong growth. To prevent the cut ends from rotting – and rhizome rot is certainly not uncommon, particularly in very wet weather – they should be dusted with Bordeaux powder before replanting them horizontally, and at the same depth at which they were previously growing.

Dividing Tuberous-rooting Types

At some time or another we've all seen the rooted tubers of a dahlia, those familiar, swollen organs which contain the stores of nutrients essential for healthy growth. Yet we may not have noticed that they are somewhat different from other tuberous varieties, in that they do not possess any growth buds. Consequently, when they are divided, the operation must be done so that each resultant portion contains one or several tubers, and, even more important, a piece of the original stem. All you have to do is make an upward cut between the adjoining root tubers, and if there is only one stem, this cut should be continued upwards and lengthwise through the stem, so that the latter is split into two as well.

Tuberous varieties such as the Jerusalem artichoke, the potato and certain begonias which carry some buds or eyes, must be split up slightly differently. These thickened sections should be cut straight across with a very sharp

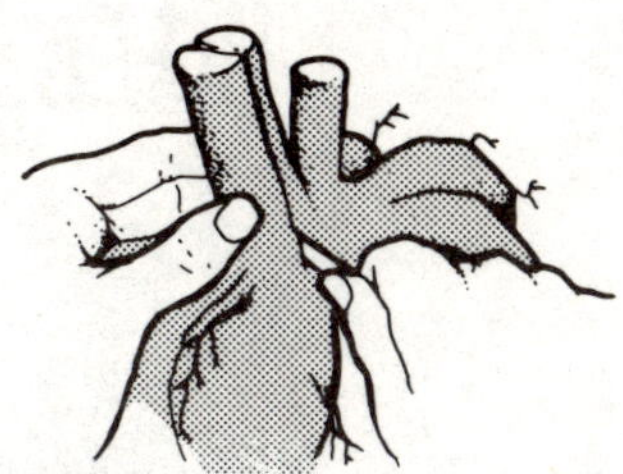

Division of a dahlia tuber.

knife, in such a way as to ensure that each severed piece contains at least one growth bud and some roots.

Other plants which you might also like to try propagating by division, are the paeony, the *mirabilis jalapa*, and the *salvia patens*.

10. LAYERING

Layering – which, by the way, must not be mistaken for an entirely different form of propagation, that of air-layering – is not a man-made means of rearing new specimens. Indeed, it is one of nature's own ways of doing the job, and the only reason we involve ourselves at all is that by selecting and encouraging suitable healthy plants to root, as they might do of their own accord later on, we can aid and speed up the process.

Many weeping forms of shrubs and trees such as the forsythia, and *Salix* (willow), reproduce quite naturally in this way, and if you know a garden which has been allowed to run amuck and become completely wild and overgrown, you will see upon closer inspection, that varieties like the border carnation, the erica, rhododendron, azalea, chaenomeles, and the loganberry, strawberry, and wild bramble will quite naturally reproduce by layering their lower branches. This is probably one of the most effective methods of increasing the slightly more difficult semi-hard and hardwood types, and it involves bending the selected bough or shoot so that the end few inches touch the ground. Then the plant will put down roots instinctively, and form an entirely new and independent specimen. The ideal period to layer any type of shrub is around early to late autumn, and although one can practise this type of propagating with plants such as border carnations or pinks almost any time of the year, the best months are at the height of the growing season around early to late summer.

First and foremost, you should guarantee your future plants the very best start in life, so it is important to ensure that the surrounding soil is just right for them. Poor starving soils must be fed and enriched with plenty of decomposed compost, leafmould and peat, whilst heavier

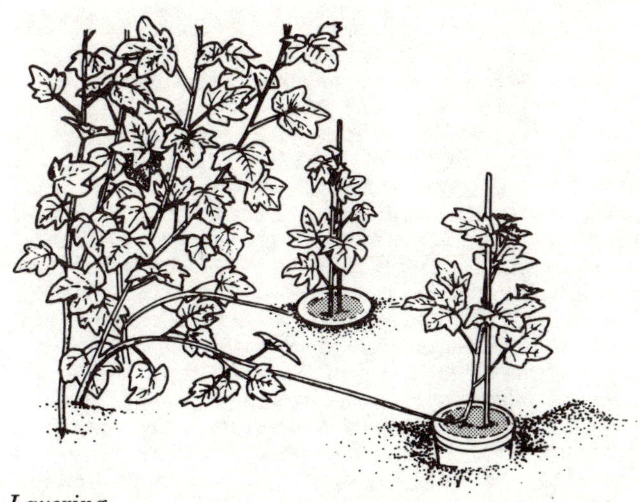

Layering.

soils should be lightened by adding some coarse sand. All this should be dug well in. That done, you will be ready to start, so arm yourself with a very sharp knife, and some layering pins, which can be purchased from most gardening shops and centres. On occasions, however, you will almost certainly run out of them when you're right in the middle of a job – it usually happens at weekends – and then will come the time to improvise with some paper clips or garden wire. When straightened out, most clips are strong enough to hold down the lighter types of plants, whilst 7.5 to 10cm (3 to 4in) lengths of slightly thicker wire can be used effectively to peg down some of the shrubs. All you have to do is double the straight wire over, and there you have your much-needed U-shaped prongs.

The types of shoots or boughs which should be chosen for this treatment are those one- to two-year-old sections which are obviously strong and healthy. When selecting a limb from a flowering plant, you should choose a specimen which is free-flowering, and the chosen portion itself should never carry either buds or blooms.

Although some varieties will root without a knife being used on any part of them, it is usually best slightly to injure the section concerned either by making an incision about two-thirds of the way through the stem, lengthwise, or by cutting and removing a small ring of bark at the point from which you wish the roots to form. Making a wound like this causes the life-giving sap to rise like a balm to the aid of the wound, and this artificially induced stimulus encourages the roots to grow. To ensure that the cut remains open, insert a tiny sliver of wood into it, and dust both the inner and surrounding area with a hormone-rooting powder. Remove some of the lower leaves, and push the wounded part under the surface of the soil. Then peg the limb down, and firm it down with more soil. It is essential to realise that the layered part is still joined to the adult plant, from which it will derive all the necessary sustenance, and this connection should only be severed when the new plant has appeared and become well and truly rooted.

That is one way of achieving the desired end; I use a slight variation. Instead of pinning the prepared limb directly into the earth, I usually almost bury a pot containing a suitable compost mixture, such as J.I.P. No. 1, alongside the adult plant, and set and peg the treated part right into the pot. This saves the extra job of having to transplant the new specimen later on, and it also reduces the chances of root damage. All I have to do is cut the adjoining stem, and lift and transfer the ready-potted plant to a cold frame. There I leave it to overwinter before planting it out the following spring.

This very effective means of propagating can, depending on the variety concerned, take either a few weeks or a few months; in the case of the rhododendron it can take anything up to a year to produce roots. Among varieties other than those already mentioned which can be successfully layered are such popular favourites as the *kalmia*, magnolia, *syringa*, camellia, clematis, mulberry, *choisya*, *pernettya*, and climbing and rambling roses.

Serpentine layering.

Serpentine Layering

The method of propagation known as serpentine layering derives its appropriate name from the Latin word *serpo*, meaning to creep. Although the method involves the same principles as those applied to ordinary layering, the serpentine treatment comes when you root not just a single growth, but a series of coiling shoots, all of which are attached to the same main stem. As with so many other gardening practices, serpentine layering has been both ardently attacked and passionately praised. Some gardeners believe it to be a good thing, whilst others think that because there is more than one resulting plant, they are all bound to be poor, weak and inferior. However, surely very much depends on the condition of the parent plant in the first instance, and the subsequent care devoted to the growing plantlets? Anyway, if one can rear a number of healthy and vigorous plants in exactly the same space of time, then it can't be too bad, and I always suggest that gardeners only use those mature plants which are in the very peak of condition.

Some climbing vines and the blackberry are frequently layered in this fashion, yet probably the most popular plant of all to be given this treatment is the clematis. The operation should be carried out at the height of the growing season, about early to mid-summer, by first selecting a young and strong outer branch. Then a series of shallow, slanting cuts between one and two inches long are made at intervals along the stem, each cut being just below or very near to a node or leaf joint. Personally, I never tempt providence by sapping the strength of the treated stem unnecessarily, so I usually limit these cuts to three or four. This way I avoid a string of weak and puny plants. Each partially severed section should be layered and pinned down, either directly into the surrounding soil, or into specially prepared pots containing the usual sandy-type rooting mixture. The 'wounded' sections must be planted just below soil level, and by the early autumn, the well established plantlets can be separated and potted or repotted, whichever the case may be, into a suitable growing medium such as J.I.P. No. 1. They will need to be overwintered within the protective walls of a cold frame, before finally being planted out in the late spring of the following year.

11. AIR-LAYERING

Usually there are disadvantages with any kind of job, and yet, when it comes to my line I consider myself one of the fortunate few to whom this general comment really doesn't apply! Of course, there are bound to be certain pitfalls when one's whole business life is wrapped up in the rearing of, and the writing about plants, because once the greenhouse and conservatory are filled to bursting point one is very inclined to fill any available living space inside the home! Inevitably there must come a time when a general clean-out of the lesser varieties is a must, and most people start with those tall and top-heavy looking wonders which, with regularly falling lower leaves, have lost their charm.

Recently I spotted such an outcast under tons of household refuse, and all the visible foliage looked burned, as if it had lived its very sad, and perhaps limited life in close proximity to a radiator. Now that it had finally lost much of its original healthy appeal, it had been discarded without so much as a second thought. There are probably numerous varieties all over the country which are about to be given the boot, and yet this seems unnecessary, when, with some patience and a little know-how, they could be restored to their former beauty. For instance, this discarded plant – a Swiss Cheese Plant (*Monstera*) – could have been successfully air-layered. After all, it seemed healthy enough, as might any other thick and woody-stemmed specimen, such as the various types of *Philodendron*, *Ficus*, and *Dracaena* the *Aralia*, and outdoor varieties like the honeysuckle, magnolia, clematis, and wistaria.

Air-layering, or ringing as it is sometimes called, is both a means of improving the overall appearance of over-tall and lanky specimens, and an effective method of propagat-

Air-layering a Swiss Cheese plant.

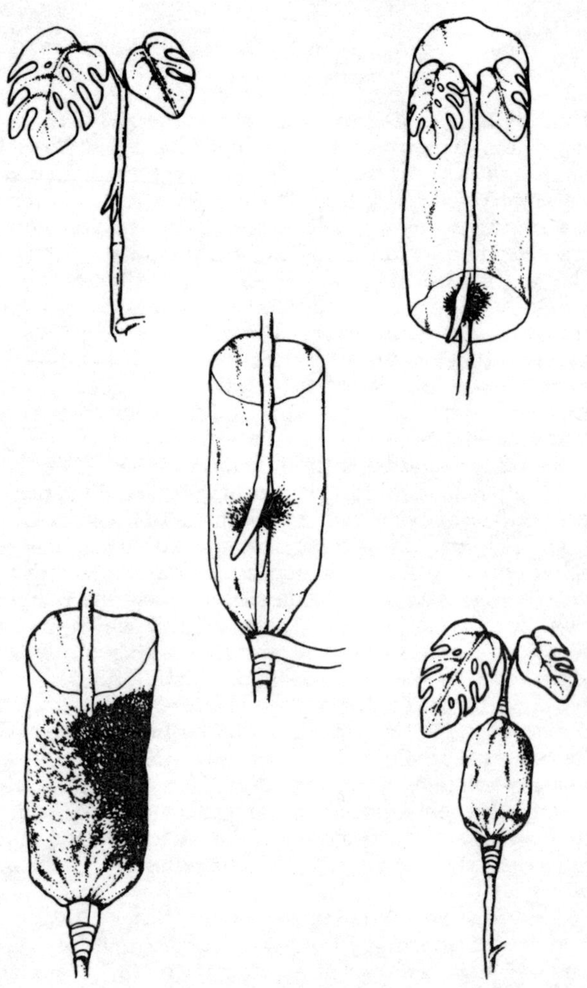

ing, by which the original specimen becomes two rooted and independent plants. This is very simply accomplished either by making a vertical incision 2.5 to 5cm (1 or 2in) long in the stem, or by removing a ring of the outer bark at the height to which you wish to reduce your plant using a sharp knife. In other words, if you want to reduce your specimen's height by 30cm (12in) then the cut or ringing should be made at that distance from the top. A cut, unlike the ringing method, must be gently prized open and kept so with a small sliver of wood – a piece of matchstick will do the job nicely, if you wedge it in. Next, dust the exposed cut or ring area thoroughly, both in and around the wound, with a hormone rooting powder, and then pack it with a well-moistened wad of sphagnum-moss. The object now is to keep the whole treated section moist. This is very important indeed, and the most efficient method is to bind the whole with a length or 'sleeve' of wide transparent polythene. Secure it firmly, but not too tightly, at the top and bottom with raffia or string so that the entire bandaged area is completely air-tight.

Now treat the plant in exactly the same way as you would do normally. Within a few weeks (although the period can vary according to each individual variety, the conditions under which it lives, and the time of the year) fine white roots will be visible through the 'see-through' wrapping. Only then should the top covering of polythene be removed. Still retaining the wadding, cut the stem right through just below the new roots, and pot this newly rooted section in a sterilised potting compost such as J.I.P. No. 2. Don't worry about the remainder of the decapitated plant, because, although it looks somewhat bare and lifeless at first, with normal care it will revive and sprout new growth fairly quickly.

All garden varieties which have undergone this treatment should be hardened-off in a cold frame before finally being transplanted out in your chosen plot.

12. RUNNERS

I have often wondered why these small and individual-to-be plants were ever christened runners, for they neither run nor walk anywhere. Although they certainly appear to be in a bit of a hurry, they are merely stretching out in search of new territory, so that they can put down their roots and establish themselves in their own right. And all this happens whilst they are still connected to the mature parent by a thread or chord – rather like an umbilical cord. If you have ever seen, for example an adult strawberry plant, or a patch of mint which has been left to ramble you will surely have noticed the baby rooted runners round about.

Certain plants, two of the better known ones being the Spider Plant (*Chlorophytum*) and the Mother-of-Thousands (*Saxifraga*), are to be seen growing in the wild surrounded by several generations all of them within an arm's length of the 'mother'. When reared as houseplants it is these babies which give us the gorgeous cascading effects which are so desirable in a wall display. However, varieties like these were endowed with this particular trait, not to satisfy our aesthetic whims, but as a means of perpetuating the species.

To help propagate these young plants, they should be encouraged to root by pinning them down by their 'necks' into small pots containing a suitable compost such as J.I.P. No. 1. They can be held in place with either 'make-do' U-shaped hair-pins, or some specially produced gardening pins or pegs. Once these babies are secured to the soil, they will quickly produce roots, and when they are well and truly rooted, the umbilical threads may be severed with a sharp knife. In their natural habitat this severance is naturally effected by the rain which slowly rots the connecting cord.

Runners on a Spider Plant.

13. SUCKERS

You will see when you read the chapter on grafting, p. 58, that I have recommended that all suckers which appear from the roots of any grafted tree or shrub should, without exception, be quickly removed, otherwise they may well sap the strength of the parent and outgrow and stultify the graft itself. The suckers will always have the same characteristics as the original stock, and will not bear those of the grafted scion. For this reason there is normally little point in propagating the suckers of such grafted fruit-bearing trees as the plum, apple or pear, or shrubs like the lilac and rose. When more original root stock is needed, or when one wants to propagate true varieties such as the *Berberis*, or *Kerria*, then this is surely one of the easiest and most convenient methods. Usually, suckers will have produced a fairly good root growth of their own within one or two years, and in the autumn or spring they can be cut with a sharp knife or pair of secateurs as close to the parent as possible. However, with varieties like the raspberry, the suckers of which are inclined to surface some distance from the parent, the necessary course of action is not always quite as straightforward as it first appears! Such varieties can be lifted, each with a few roots attached, but only the strongest ones should be used and replanted into a permanent growing position.

14. BULBS AND CORMS

When I was in my early teens, I had very good reason to remember accidentally slicing into several muscari and lilium bulbs with a hoe, when they were growing together in a flower border. At the time, I was concerned that I had caused them irrevocable harm. When I came to lift them after the foliage had died down, it was another story, for I was astonished and thrilled to find that the scarred muscari bulbs had developed minute bulb-like growths in between the scales, whilst the damaged liliums had given birth to bulblets fairly close to the soil level. I had come across this form of propagation before, but never after a bulb had been injured, and in the autumn those bulblets were removed and potted up.

It could be Nature's way of ensuring that wounded adult bulbs give birth to more youngsters before they come to the end of their productive lives. Alternatively, this forming of bulbs just might be a means of callousing and protecting the cut, so as to aid the bulb's recovery, in much the same way as we grow a scab and a hard skin over a wound. However, it is generally accepted that the flow of life-giving sap is activated by any sort of blow or bruising, as I mentioned in the chapters on budding and grafting. For this reason many bulb nurserymen don't just wait for offsets to form naturally, but hurry up the process by artificially inducing them, by scraping and scuffing the base of the mature bulb, from which both roots and bulblets eventually appear. Hyacinths are a special case where the method is of great help, because if left alone, they are not inclined to reproduce very easily.

Garlic, the offsets of which grow attached to the mother bulb, is produced in much the same fashion, and the bulblets, called cloves, are usually detached and crushed into a variety of gorgeous dishes. But instead of cooking

Bulb offsets.

them, you can set each clove, complete with its outer casing, into the soil where they will produce whole bulbs of garlic to titillate your taste buds. You should remove the flowers as they form if you want to harvest the bulbs for culinary purposes.

Offsets

Offsets are a reliable means of rearing new stock, because they usually breed and flower true to type. They may be detached from the parent bulb after the foliage has died down at the beginning of the dormancy period. In most cases they can be removed quite easily by hand. With tulips, for instance, you may well come across some which have developed rather lower than the others; these are frequently referred to as 'droppers', and are just as good as the rest.

After grading according to size, and labelling them, you can plant them out into beds, where they will take at least a couple of years to reach flowering maturity. Once nearly full-grown, they can be replanted into a permanent growing site.

Hyacinths

As I mentioned before, hyacinths are very loath to reproduce when left to their own devices. But at the end of the resting period, just before they start to sprout, they can be induced to give birth by either gouging out a small section of the bulb or making several cuts in the base where the roots form.

Each bulb prepared thus can then be planted in moist sand, and given a temperature of about 64°F (18°C). Keep the compost nicely damp, but otherwise leave them untouched for the remainder of the growing season, during which time they should produce a number of bulblets. These can be safely left until the autumn when they should be potted up separately and grown on in the usual way.

This method is usually practised only by the professional grower, but if you have a way with plants, plenty of patience, and a couple of spare bulbs which you would like to try to propagate, then go ahead, and I wish you the very best of luck!

Bulbils

These are small and immature growths which form in between the leaf axils of certain varieties of tulips and liliums. Strains of lilies which reproduce in this way include the white flowering *L. sargentiae*, the *L. tigrinum* which has typical orange-spotted, tiger-like heads, and the hardy *L. bulbiferum*, a popular strain of which is the tangerine and trumpet-shaped *L. bulbiferum croceum*.

Bulbils can be removed gently by hand when the foliage starts to turn yellow around early autumn.

Once detached, they can be potted up singly into 7.5cm (3in) pots, or set in boxes of J.I.P. seed compost, or set in a mixture of 3 parts of J.I.P. No. 1., to 1 part of peat. Plant them at a depth of 1cm (½in) and space them about 5cm (2in) apart. When they are large enough to handle with ease, transfer them individually into small pots of J.I.P.

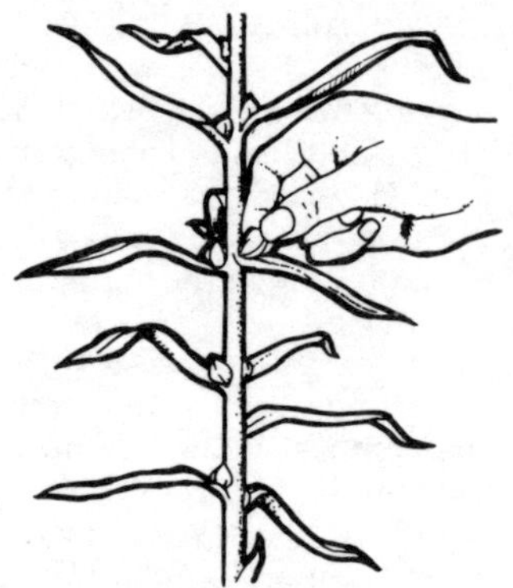

Bulbils.

No. 1, and place them in a cold frame. With the arrival of warmer weather they can again be transferred, this time outside into a suitable bed, where they should reach flowering adulthood within two to three years. When fully mature, they can be planted in their permanent growing position.

Corms

Gladioli reproduce in much the same way as do many other bulbs, and when the late autumn arrives many minute cormlets will be seen forming on top and around the sides of the older corms. To propagate these, you must start when the flowering gladioli are fading and the foliage is fast becoming withered and discoloured. Then the adult plants are ready to be lifted, and once the soil is shaken from them, and the main stem is severed just above each corm, the exhausted and shrivelled oldest corms should be thrown away. The remaining younger cormlets, which can be easily detached with the fingers, should be left in a warm, dry place, for about a week until they themselves are dry, when they can be safely stored in boxes of sand in a cool, frost-free shed.

During the following spring, these cormlets should be

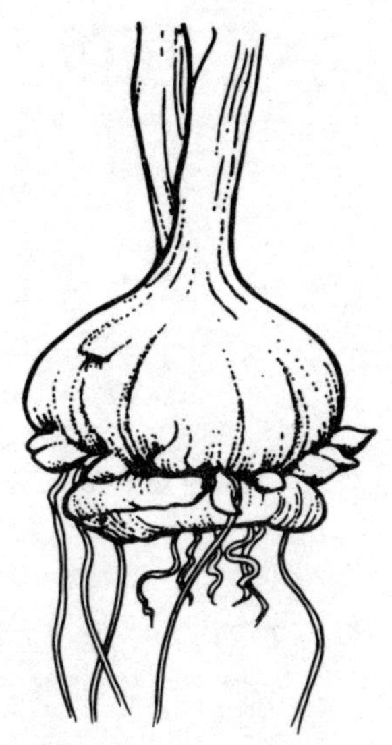

Gladiolus corm.

planted 7.5cm (3in) deep in drills, the floors of which should contain a thin layer of sand. Although only a few will flower during the first year – and that's if you're lucky – the growing area must still be kept free from weeds, and the whole process of lifting and storing them must be repeated in the coming autumn. If all goes well, and there's no reason why it shouldn't, your corms should reach full flowering maturity within two or three years.

15. A GUIDE TO PLANT, SHRUB AND TREE PROPAGATION

Abutilon From seed sown in late winter and stem cuttings taken in early autumn.

Acacia From seed sown in early spring and semi-ripe cuttings taken in summer.

Achillea By division of roots in early spring or by seed sown in early spring.

Achimenes By division of tubers in early spring.

Aconitum By division of roots from autumn to early spring.

Actinidia By seed sown in autumn.

Agapanthus By division of roots in early spring and by seed sown in spring.

Ailanthus By root suckers in late summer.

Alstroemeria By seed sown in early spring and by division in early spring.

Amaranthus By seed sown in early spring.

Anchusa By root cuttings or seed, depending on the strain.

Anemone (spring flowering) By offsets or division in late summer and by seed sown in late summer.
(summer and autumn flowering) By division from autumn to early spring and by root cuttings between late autumn and winter.

Aquilegia By seed sown in summer and by division from autumn to early spring.

Arbutus By seed sown in early spring and by heel cuttings of half-ripe wood in summer.

Asparagus fern By division in early spring and by seed sown in spring.

Azalea simsii By half-ripe cuttings in early summer.

Bamboo By seed and by division, in late spring.

Berberis By seed sown in late autumn and by heel cuttings in late summer.

Bougainvillea By half-ripe cuttings in summer.

Browallia By seed sown in early spring or late summer.

Brunfelsia By cuttings of partially ripe wood from early spring to late summer.

Buddleia By half-ripe heel cuttings in summer.

Buxus By cuttings in late summer and early autumn.

Calceolaria (bedding and pot plants) By seed (the time varying according to the strain) and by heel cuttings in late summer.

Camellia By half-ripe cuttings from early summer to late summer, by layering in late summer/early autumn and by leaf bud cuttings from early summer to late summer.

Campanula By seed sown in autumn or spring, by division in autumn and by cuttings in late spring.

Canna By seed sown in late winter and by division in early spring.

Carnations (annuals) By seed sown from spring to early summer.

(border) By seed sown from spring to early summer or by layering in summer.

(perpetual flowering) By cuttings taken from side-shoots from early winter to late winter and by seed sown in winter.

Caryopteris By half-ripe cuttings taken in late summer/early autumn.

Catalpa By half-ripe heel cuttings taken in summer.

Celosia By seed sown in late winter/early spring.

Cercis By seed sown in early spring.

Chimonanthus By seed sown in early autumn and by layering in late summer/early autumn.

Chrysanthemum (alpine species) By cuttings in summer.
(annual species) By seed sown in early spring and by cuttings of side-shoots from early autumn to late winter.
(perennial species) By division in early spring and by basal shoot cuttings in spring.

Cineraria By seed sown from spring to late summer.

Clematis (climbers) By half-ripe stem cuttings in summer, by seed sown in autumn and by layering in early spring.
(herbaceous) By basal cuttings taken in spring and by division from autumn to early spring.

Clivia By seed, when ripe, or as soon as purchased, and by division in spring.

Coleus By seed sown in late winter and by cuttings taken in late summer or spring.

Coreopsis (annuals) By seed sown from spring to early summer.
(perennials) By division from autumn to early spring and by seed sown in spring.

Cotoneaster By ripe heel-cuttings in late summer/early autumn, by half-ripe cuttings in summer, by layering in autumn and by seed sown in early autumn.

Cydonia By hardwood cuttings with a heel, taken in autumn, or by layering in early autumn.

Cytisus By seed sown in spring and by heel cuttings in late summer.

Dahlia (border) By division of the tubers in early spring.
(bedding) By seed sown in early spring.

Daphne By heel cuttings taken from summer to early autumn and by seed sown when ripe.

Delphinium By basal cuttings in spring, by division in early spring, by seed sown in spring or early autumn.

Deutzia By hardwood cuttings taken in autumn or by partially ripe cuttings in summer.

Dielytra or *Dicentra* By division between autumn and early spring, by seed sown in early spring and by root cuttings taken in early spring.

Dierama By seed sown in early spring and by offsets in autumn.

Digitalis By seed sown in late spring/early summer.

Dipladenia By heel cuttings taken in spring.

Disanthus By half-ripe heel cuttings taken in summer and by layering in early autumn.

Dracaena By basal shoots with some stem cutting attached, taken in spring.

Dryas By heel cuttings in late summer or spring, by seed sown in early autumn and by division in early spring.

Epimedium By seed sown in summer or by division from early autumn to early spring.

Eremurus By division of roots in early autumn or by seed before early spring.

Erica By cuttings taken in early spring.

Erigeron By seed sown in spring and by division from autumn to early spring.

Eryngium By seed sown in early spring, by root cuttings taken in late winter and by division in early spring.

Escallonia By half-ripe heel cuttings taken in late summer/early autumn.

Eucalyptus By seed sown in spring.

Euonymus By seed sown in early autumn and by heel cuttings taken in late summer.

Forsythia By cuttings of present season's growth taken in autumn and by layering in autumn.

Fothergilla By layering in early autumn.

Fraxinus By seed sown in autumn.

Fremontia By seed sown in spring.

Fuchsia By tip cuttings in early spring and by seed sown in spring.

Gaillardia By seed sown under glass in early spring, or outdoors in late spring/early summer.

Gardenia By heel cuttings taken in early spring.

Garrya By semi-ripe heel cuttings taken in late summer/early autumn or by layering in early autumn.

Genista By heel cuttings taken in late summer and by seed sown in early spring.

Geranium By seed sown from early autumn to early spring and by division between early autumn and early spring.

Gerbera By seed sown in late winter and early spring and by division in early spring.

Ginkgo By ripe seed sown any time from spring to autumn.

Gladiolus By seed sown in early spring and by cormlets set in early spring.

Griselinia By heel cuttings taken in late summer.

Haemanthus By offsets in early spring.

Hamamelis By layering in early autumn, by heel cuttings in early autumn and by ripe seed in autumn.

Helenium By division between autumn and spring.

Helianthus By seed sown in early spring; by division of perennials between autumn and early spring.

Hemerocallis By division between autumn and spring.

Hibiscus (shrubby varieties) By heel cuttings taken in summer.
(annual varieties) By seed sown in spring.
(greenhouse varieties) By heel cuttings taken between spring and late summer.

Hosta By division in early spring.

Hydrangea (shrubby types) By cuttings taken in late summer/early autumn.
(climbing types) By cuttings taken in early summer.

Hypericum By soft cuttings taken in late spring/early summer.

Ilex By layering in autumn and by heel cuttings taken in late summer.

Incarvillea By division in autumn and by seed sown in early spring.

Jacobinia By cuttings taken in spring.

Jasminum By cuttings of partially ripe wood with a node, during late summer/early autumn.

Juncus By division during the spring.

Juniperus By ripe seed sown in early autumn and by heel cuttings taken in the autumn.

Kalmia By layering of present season's growth during late summer/early autumn and by semi-ripe cuttings taken in late summer.

Kerria By cuttings taken in late summer/early autumn and by division from autumn to early spring.

Kniphofia By seed sown in spring and by division in spring.

Kochia By seed sown in early spring.

Laburnum By seed sown in autumn and by grafting in early spring.

Laelia By division from late winter to late spring.

Lampranthus By stem cuttings taken in late summer/early autumn and by seed sown in spring.

Lantana By seed sown in late winter and by cuttings taken in late summer.

Lapageria By layering in spring and by seed sown in early spring.

Larix By seed sown in early spring and by tip cuttings taken in summer.

Laurus By heel cuttings taken in late summer/early autumn and by layering in summer.

Lavendula By ripe cuttings taken in late summer/early autumn.

Leptospermum By half-ripe cuttings in early summer.

Lewisia By offsets taken in early summer and by seed sown in early spring.

Liatris By division in early spring and by seed sown in early spring.

Lilium By ripe seed sown in early autumn, by scale propagation in early autumn or early spring and by division from autumn to early spring.

Liriope By division in early spring.

Lobelia By seed sown in early spring. The herbaceous varieties may also be divided in early spring.

Lonicera (hardy varieties) By layering from late summer to late autumn, by seed sown in early autumn, by hardwood cuttings taken in early autumn and by stem cuttings taken in summer.

Lupinus By seed sown in early spring and by cuttings taken in early spring.

Lysimachia By division from autumn to early spring.

Lythrum By division from autumn to spring, by seed sown in spring and by basal cuttings taken in spring.

Magnolia By heel cuttings of semi-ripened wood taken in summer, by layering in spring and by seed sown in autumn.

Mahonia By ripe seeds sown in late summer and by tip cuttings taken in summer.

Malus By seed or grafting in early spring.

Maurandia By seed sown in late winter/early spring and by cuttings taken in late winter or late summer.

Mazus By division in spring or early autumn.

Meconopsis By seed sown in late summer or spring.

Medlar By ripe seed sown in early autumn or by grafting and budding in summer.

Mertensia By ripe seed sown in summer or by division in autumn or early spring.

Mimosa By seed sown in early spring.

Mimulus By seed, sown in late winter for certain strains and spring for others, by cuttings taken in spring and by division in early spring.

Mulberry By cuttings taken in autumn or spring.

Muscari By division after flowering has ceased or by seed sown in summer and early autumn.

Myosotis By seed sown in spring.

Myrtus By heel cuttings taken in early summer.

Nerine By ripe seed sown in late spring and by offsets or division in late summer.

Nerium By seed sown in spring or by half-ripe cuttings taken in summer.

Nigella By seed sown in early spring.

Nyssa By layering in the autumn and by seed sown in autumn.

Olearia By half-ripe cuttings taken in late summer

Ornithogalum By bulbils planted in summer or by seed sown in early autumn.

Osmanthus By half-ripe cuttings taken in summer or by layering in early autumn.

Oxalis By division in early spring.

Paeonia By seed sown in early autumn, by layering in early spring, by hardwood cuttings taken in autumn, by grafting in summer or by division in early autumn.

Papaver (annuals) By seed sown in spring or early autumn.
(perennials) By seed sown in spring, by division in early spring and by the root cuttings of certain strains when taken during the winter.

Parrotia By seed sown in early autumn or by layering in early autumn.

Parthenocissus By layering in autumn, by seed sown in autumn, by half-ripe cuttings taken in late summer and by hardwood cuttings taken in late autumn.

Passiflora By ripe seed or by stem cuttings taken in summer.

Pelargonium By seed sown in late winter or by tip cuttings taken in early spring and summer.

Pereskia By seed sown in spring or by semi-ripe cuttings in summer.

Pernettya By seed sown in autumn or by cuttings taken in early autumn.

Perovskia By heel cuttings taken in summer.

Philadelphus By hardwood cuttings taken in autumn or by half-ripe cuttings taken in summer.

Phormium By seed sown in early spring or by division in spring.

Physalis By seed sown in spring or by division in spring.

Picea By seed sown in early spring.

Pieris By seed sown in early spring or late autumn, by half-ripe cuttings taken in late summer or by layering in early autumn.

Pinus By seed sown in early spring and by grafting in early spring.

Pittosporum By seed sown in early spring or by half-ripe heel cuttings taken in summer.

Pleione By offsets in spring.

Plumbago By basal shoot cuttings taken in spring or by heel cuttings taken in summer.

Podophyllum By ripe seed sown in early spring or summer or by division in early spring.

Polypodium By division in spring.

Polystichum By spores sown in early spring or by division in early spring.

Pteris By spores sown in early spring.

Pulmonaria By seed sown in spring, or by division in autumn or early spring.

Pulsatilla By seed sown in summer.

Pyracantha By hardwood cuttings taken in autumn, by ripe seed sown in autumn or by cuttings taken in summer.

Pyrethrum By seed sown in early spring or by division in early spring.

Quince By layering in early autumn or by hardwood heel cuttings taken in autumn.

Ramonda By seed sown in early autumn or early spring and by leaf cuttings taken in early summer.

Raoulia By division from summer to early autumn.

Rechsteineria By seed sown in early spring, by basal cuttings taken in spring or by division of tubers in early spring.

Rheum By seed sown in early spring or by division from late autumn to late winter.

Rhododendron By seed sown in early spring, by layering almost any time of the year, by cuttings taken in summer, by half-ripe cuttings taken in early summer or by saddle grafting.

Rhus By layering in early spring or by half-ripe heel cuttings taken in summer.

Ricinus By seed sown in early spring.

Robinia By seed sown in early spring or by planting out rooted suckers between autumn and later winter.

Romneya By root cuttings taken in late winter or by seed sown in early spring.

Rose By seed sown in autumn; by budding in summer.

Rubus By division from autumn to early spring, by layering in late summer or by semi-hardwood cuttings taken in late summer.

Rudbeckia By seed sown in early spring, or by division from autumn to early spring.

Ruellia By basal cuttings taken in spring.

Saintpaulia By leaf cuttings taken from late spring to early autumn and by seed sown in early spring.

Salix By hardwood cuttings taken from autumn to early spring.

Salpiglossis By seed sown in early spring.

Salvia By seed sown in early spring.

Sambucus By half-ripe heel cuttings taken in summer or by hardwood cuttings taken in autumn.

Sansevieria By suckers during the growing months or by leaf cuttings taken from spring to late summer.

Santolina By half-ripe side shoots taken in summer.

Saponaria (perennials) By seed sown in early spring and by division or by runners from autumn to early spring.

Scabiosa (perennials) By division in early spring or by basal cuttings taken in spring.
(annuals) By seed sown in the spring.

Schefflera By seed sown in late winter/early spring.

Scilla By ripe seed sown in the summer or by offsets when all flowering has ceased.

Sedum (indoor varieties) By leaf cuttings any time during the growing period, by division from spring to late summer, by stem cuttings taken between spring and early autumn and by seed sown in spring.
(outdoor varieties) By division from autumn to early spring, by stem cuttings from early spring to late summer and by seed sown in spring.

Sempervivum By seed sown in early spring or by offsets replanted from spring to early autumn.

Sequoia By seed sown in early spring or by tip cuttings of suckers taken in early autumn.

Sinningia By seed sown in early spring, by basal shoots taken in spring, by division in early spring and by leaf cuttings taken in summer.

Skimmia By ripe seed sown in early autumn or by half-ripe heel cuttings taken in summer.

Solanum By seed sown in early spring and by side cuttings taken in summer.

Solidago By division from autumn to early spring.

Sonerila By seed sown in spring or by basal cuttings taken in late spring/early summer.

Sorbus By ripe seed sown in autumn.

Sparaxis By seed sown in early spring or late summer and by offsets replanted any time during the growing period.

Spathiphyllum By division in spring.

Spiraea By division from autumn to early spring, by hardwood cuttings taken in autumn and by half-ripe cuttings taken in summer.

Sprekelia By offsets in early spring.

Stachys By division from autumn to early spring.

Stephanandra By hardwood cuttings taken in autumn or rooted suckers taken from autumn to early spring.

Stephanotis By cuttings from spring to early summer.

Sternbergia By offsets taken in late summer.

Stipa By division in early spring.

Syringa By half-ripe heel cuttings taken during the summer.

Tagetes By seed sown in early spring.

Tamarix By hardwood cuttings taken in autumn.

Taxodium By seed sown in early spring.

Taxus By lateral shoots with a heel taken in early autumn or by seed sown in autumn.

Thuja By tip cuttings taken in early autumn, or by seed sown in late winter/early spring.

Thymus By division in early spring or early autumn or by heel cuttings taken in summer.

Trollius By division in spring or early autumn and by ripe seed sown from early autumn to early spring.

Tropaeolum (annuals) By seed sown in spring.
(perennials) By division in early spring, or by division of tubers during the spring.

Tulip By offsets set in summer, by ripe seed sown in late summer.

Ursinia By seed sown in early spring.

Verbascum (alpine species) By heel cuttings taken in late spring/early summer.
(border species) By seed sown in spring.

Verbena By seed sown in early spring or by root division in spring.

Veronica (alpine species) By division in early spring or by cuttings taken in summer.
(herbaceous perennials) By division in early spring.

Viburnum By layering in early autumn, by seed sown in early autumn or by heel cuttings taken in early summer.

Viola By basal cuttings taken in summer, by seed sown in early spring or summer (depending on the variety).

Weigela By cuttings taken in autumn or by half-ripe heel cuttings taken in early summer.

Wistaria By grafting in early spring, by heel cuttings taken in late summer, by layering in late spring and by seed sown in early spring.

Yucca By rooted suckers in early spring.

Zantedeschia By division of rhizomes or by offsets, either in autumn or late winter – depending on the variety.

Zinnia By seed sown in early spring.

INDEX